MW01289806

THE 12 DROP RULE
GETTING THE MOST OUT OF
WINE AND LIFE

Patrick Drinan

Copyright © 2014 Patrick Drinan
All rights reserved.

ISBN 1502356627
ISBN 9781502356628
Library of Congress Control Number: 2014916500
CreateSpace Independent Publishing Platform
North Charleston, South Carolina

Contents

FOREWORD

We have heard that "the unexamined life is not worth living," but obsession and examination are different things. Lying awake at night playing insomnia Jeopardy with worries or regrets is hardly the good life. In our highly materialistic society, it's worth reviving a cultural conversation about the nature of the good life, beyond having enough money for expenses and retirement or keeping up with the Joneses.

I had the pleasure of meeting Pat Drinan and his wife, Mary Ann, in 2012 while giving them a special tour of the wineries in the Monticello American Viticultural Area (AVA) near Charlottesville, Virginia, where Pat had attended graduate school at the University of Virginia years earlier. I gave them an autographed copy of my book on Virginia wine, *Beyond Jefferson's Vines*, and we enjoyed discussing how Thomas Jefferson would have viewed the evolution of today's wine industry, even as we enjoyed visiting the local wineries. I'm very pleased that Pat's book project, which he told me about then, has come to fruition and that his visit to Virginia wine country helped inspire it, and I am honored to introduce you to this fine book.

If you enjoy wine or philosophy, you may have noticed that there is a frequent mention of each when people are experiencing the other. As a young man contemplating work in the wine industry, I remember reading *The Fireside Book of Wine*, Alexis Bespaloff's great anthology of wine quotations from antiquity to the present, and being impressed by the persistence of the link between philosophy and wine over thousands of years.

You may have heard that the origin of the Greek symposium was a ritual called *cottabus*, in which men (women had the bacchanal) sat around drinking wine and trying to be witty, attempting to find the ideal balance between too little and too much wine and to say just the right thing for the moment. Academic symposia today might benefit from the application of more wine. As the Greeks were trying to demonstrate, it wasn't getting indiscriminately drunk that was the goal, nor staying too sober to fully enjoy the company, but finding that balance.

Accordingly, I was delighted to see Pat's book draft and to learn how this book reintroduces the symposium concept in the subtitle: "Getting the Most Out of Wine and Life." Haven't we all wanted to do that? And here's a (not too large) book to show us how!

I'm also intrigued by the notions of the "12 drop experience," creating a "new cottabus," and constructing a "personal terroir." The consumption of fine wine has seemed by its nature to give us pause as the rich yet refreshing nectar fills our palates, inspiring us to reflect on the miracle that transforms the ordinary (grape juice) into the extraordinary. I like how Pat moves from the "12 drop rule" to the playful yet transformative drama of the "12 drop experience." After all, wine has an honored place in the ritual of religions. Notwithstanding the abstemious sensibilities of teetotalers, Christ both began and ended his ministry with miracles of wine. Pat's use of Epicurus, the Greek philosopher (circa 300 BC), and Thomas Jefferson of the Enlightenment having a Socratic-style dialogue shows the continuity with which wine and philosophy are linked in the Western mind. He explains how their sensibilities about wine, life, and philosophy were remarkably in tune and makes it all relevant with the concept of "practical wisdoms" we can choose for ourselves to guide our lives.

At the heart of the playful yet contemplative art of creating a "new cottabus" to make sense of wine and life is intentionally celebrating the blessings of the present moment, which is easy to do with fine wine and the company of fine friends; as Pat writes, "It is identifying a moment and finding fullness in it." This book already has made me begin to think of "practical wisdoms" for my own life, ranging from the profound ("We are alive to the extent we are grateful") to the blunt and earthy ("Life is short. Don't be a d–k").

When you think about it, drinking wine and savoring the experience either alone or with friends are pleasures that have changed very little in thousands of years, while the world changes constantly around us and even the way we interact with other people has become virtual and disconnected. This book offers a rewarding, challenging, yet fun way to be in, and celebrate, the present moment in the way the ancients did, sharing practical wisdoms with our friends without the need for the latest app. And for those of you who have not yet discovered the fine wines of Virginia's Monticello AVA, Pat includes an appendix of tasting notes to show you that Jefferson's winegrowing heirs are doing him proud. May you enjoy the journey, and, just as Thomas Jefferson and Epicurus affirmed the place of fine wine in the good life, let us toast with them and like-minded souls: To life!

Richard Leahy
Charlottesville, Virginia
December 2014

PREFACE

This is a self-help book. It is designed to help lovers of fine wines explore their own character and those of their friends.

The specific object of this exploration is to help you create and clarify a set of individualized practical wisdoms that define you and propel you to a better self. It is about listening to and shaping your own "personal terroir," your landscape of commitments and your philosophy of living that is as important to you as landscape, microclimate, and winemaking skill are to producing fine wines. It is also about arts of conversation and designing a new wine ritual—what I have come to call the *new cottabus*—modeled on the ancient Greek game played at philosophical symposia.

Why practical wisdoms? Because practical wisdoms are dispositions to action that are windows on who you are and what animates you. They are the maxims and principles you rely on in everyday life. These reliances are key to understanding not only yourself, but also relationships among family members, friends, and colleagues. Once you can be explicit about your reliances and your preferred set of practical wisdoms, you gain a clarity, focus, and mindfulness that can enrich life on many dimensions.

Additionally, this book is an ode to sacred geographies—wine regions that can have a compelling quality because of gratifications and sanctuary that are both offered and realized. The sacred geography of a wine region is a place that is "right" for you—where you can nurture the sensibilities that bring out the best in you. It is about more than wine tourism—it is about embracing a more textured and rounded understanding of your personal terroir. A marriage of personal terroir and sacred geography can be very pleasurable and exceptionally gratifying.

The Monticello appellation around Charlottesville, Virginia, marketed as the "birthplace of American wines," is that sacred geography for me. But it could be any wine region that inspires a lover of wine and lover of thinking. As I write this book 3,000 miles from Virginia, I understand the lure and promise of even distant sacred geographies. May your sacred geography be close in mind as you ponder your personal terroir, your landscape of practical wisdoms.

Although I am a retired professor, this book is not written for a narrow academic audience. It is part travelogue (France and Virginia) and part reflection, in a journalistic style, from notes on the pools of wisdom I could tap from our general culture and conversations with many people including friends, academic colleagues, and wine professionals. It is a result of a meditative posture and a compulsive curiosity about how to find meaning in everyday life. I take full responsibility for any errors of presentation, even as I am grateful to all those who showed interest in this project and provided me with advice, counsel, and often surprising encouragement.

There are many acknowledgments for this volume. In France: Anne Parent, Bernard Muller, Ann Lavirotte, and Celine Dandelot. In Virginia: Richard Leahy, Dennis Horton, Dee Allison, James King, Michael E. Bowles, Charlie Grisham, Lee Reeder, Elizabeth Smith, Andrew Hodson, Brad Hansen, and Peter Hatch. In California: Jay Corey, Daniel Sheehan, Linda Peterson, Virginia Lewis, Larry Hinman, Eric von Ehrenberg, Tricia Bertram Gallant, Jamie Gallant, Julie and Jacques Corpora, Art and Lori Perez, Linda Rogers, Donna Drinan, Jessica Watshke, Frances Watson, and Rex and Kathy Warburton. Along with this cast of characters, our daughters—Christiana Gimon and Megan Fischer—provided useful input early in my research. Last, but far from least, is the co-discoverer of the 12 drop rule, my spouse of forty-seven years, Mary Ann; she has been not only a loving companion but an inspiration for me in developing a philosophy of living that is immensely satisfying. May there be many more drops in our bottle of life.

Patrick Drinan, PhD
Escondido, California
December 2014

CHAPTER 1

INTRODUCTION: DISCOVERY OF THE 12 DROP RULE AND THE SEARCH FOR A NEW COTTABUS

Whether the Cup with sweet or bitter run,
The Wine of Life keeps oozing drop by drop,
The Leaves of Life keep falling one by one.
—Omar Khayyam

The origins of the 12 drop rule are found in a vacation trip to Italy and southern France taken by my wife, Mary Ann, and me in the mid-1990s. The stage was set in Siena, one of our favorite Italian cities and home of the Palio—the famous horse race and civic celebration that has occurred in the center of the city for more than six centuries. Our vacation was thorough—no e-mail or cell phones. After a few days of relaxation and enjoyment of wine with our dinners, a kind of silliness came over us in Siena. As we finished a bottle one evening, we asked ourselves how many drops were still left after normal pouring. Our research had begun!

For the next two weeks, through northern Italy and southern France, we measured and recorded the number of remaining drops in each bottle of wine (after the normal pouring, of course). By the time we settled into our destination, Roussillon in southern France, we had established that there was always a minimum of twelve drops remaining—and frequently more. What were we going to do with this newly acquired, seemingly frivolous knowledge? We had discovered a rule that was reliable, but how to use it to tease out other reliances or rules for living? As we returned from vacation to our careers as college professors in southern California, we had little time to answer the question—although, of course, we continued to test the rule and playfully engaged friends in the exercise over congenial meals.

It was fifteen years later, approaching retirement, that we began to see the discovery of the 12 drop rule as an opportunity to be creative and attempt to answer the question we earlier had posed in Roussillon. As I took this on as my retirement project, I next had to ask if anyone else had come up with anything similar. Many people, of course, have figured out that there are a few drops left in a bottle—whether they are owners of bars, alcoholics, or teenagers taking advantage of their parents' leftovers after a party. Ellen Brown in the *Wall Street Journal* reported in late 2012 that many consumers were becoming obsessive about getting the last drops out of household and beauty products, so much so that manufacturers were responding to this obsession. For instance, ketchup makers have produced "upside down" bottles to squeeze out the last drops of the condiment. It is not only ketchup, but also an array of household products from toothpaste to shampoo. According to a package supplier cited by Brown, most consumers are now saying that getting the most out of a package is the most important quality sought in buying a product.

So getting the last drops is trendy, but was there anything like the 12 drop rule as applied to wine? Exhaustive searches of the web did not come up with candidates that could mimic the 12 drop rule. But a book gift from our older daughter—who knew my fascination with the 12 drop rule—revealed an ancient ritual and game that took advantage of the last drops of wine in a vessel. The book was a bestseller by Tom Standage, *A History of the World in 6 Glasses*, in which he briefly described the Greek tradition of a ritual called *kottabus* (or cottabus more frequently). Cottabus took place, according to Standage, as a part of a philosophical symposium as a game of "flicking the last remaining drops of wine from one's cup at a specific target, such as another person, a disk-shaped bronze target, or even a cup floating in a bowl of water, with the aim of sinking it." Now I had found something similar to the 12 drop rule, something playful but philosophically minded. Yes, there was a precedent!

Cottabus was a game that glorified skill. Success was often considered an omen of good luck in love, and frequently there were wagers on the outcome of the game itself. Cottabus flourished for about two centuries as can be seen from the many remnants of cottabus sculptures found in Italy and Greece. Cottabus died out as a game and ritual in the Roman era for reasons unknown. But it is not hard to imagine the zest of conversations as people played the game and speculated about what success or failure might mean in their lives.

Toward a New Cottabus

The purpose of this book is to devise a new cottabus, one that takes the last drops of wine in a bottle not as a game but as a trigger to conversations about, and declarations of, practical wisdoms. Whether or not this will become a meme—"an idea, behavior, or style that spreads from person to person within a culture," as Wikipedia describes it—is not yet knowable. But it certainly qualifies, in the language of the philosopher Daniel Dennett, as "a good proto-meme: a slightly obsessional—that is, oft-recurring, oft-rehearsed—little hobbyhorse of an idea." And the philosopher Alfred North Whitehead, in the same vein, has said, "Almost all new ideas have a certain aspect of foolishness when they are first produced." Exploring this "foolishness" is what this book is about. There can be foolishness in play—and in plays, as Shakespeare has shown us. But there is a delightful combination of curiosity and comedy about play that takes foolishness to new levels. Who has not watched a cricket match with a sense of wonder not only about what they were doing but why they seemed to be enjoying it?

There is much more than foolishness in play, of course. The late University of Colorado philosopher David Hawkins argued that an assumption that play is all foolishness leads to the disparagement of play.

He says that play, for children, "represents a powerful organizer of their growing experience and, at the same time, a synoptic expression of it." This kind of play can be extended into adulthood and should not be disparaged. Hawkins insisted that play can be "the matrix out of which is born the capacity for the very definition of sober and serious ends, and the capacity to reconstruct them in the course of a worthy life." And the great humanist Erasmus reminds us that "nothing is more graceful than to handle light subjects in such a way that you seem to have been anything but trifling."

This book is about taking something as playful and light as the 12 drop rule and creating structure around it. The structure—the 12 drop experience—is designed to be transformative, one of the seven play types established by the National Institute of Play. (Yes, there is such an organization!) Transformation means taking an activity through levels of imagination that lead to discovery of new knowledge—in this case about yourself and your friends, but also about wine appreciation and wine regions.

But the 12 drop rule and 12 drop experience do not constitute a game even if they turn out to be compulsive. A game implies competition, and, yes, games can certainly be compulsive. But the 12 drop experience is not designed to be competitive. It is not rule-bound like football, baseball, or golf. It is an autobiographical exercise and establishes an arena for philosophically minded conversation, including with oneself, that aspires to be inspirational. It is a marriage of self-help and establishing a radius of trust with others. It is like falling in love and refining sensibilities you knew were there and that you knew you wanted to develop. It is identifying a moment and finding fullness in it. It is like enjoying a mystery novel and not quite knowing where it is going, but seeing your own character develop instead of the characters in the novel.

It is easy to see how the practice of counting the last drops may become obsessive for some individuals. But I believe that the 12 drop experience is also a cultural opportunity to work on character in a society that often seems obsessed with self-help, yet dreads the idea that narcissism and nihilism may overwhelm our postmodern identities. The author of *I Drink Therefore I Am*, Roger Scruton, has captured the opportunity offered by wine: "It enables you to hold the problem of the self before your mind, and not fall into the Cartesian abyss." Wine invites us to be philosophically minded without pretending to be professional philosophers. And the rituals of wine appreciation provide congenial pockets of order that give an opportunity to safely explore who you are and what is most meaningful in your life—which at that moment is most likely friendship. But it deserves to be probed and made into something more—something the legal philosopher Ronald Dworken calls, in a different context, a "process of philosophical ascent." So, the irony of the 12 drop rule is that, as the last drops of wine fall into our glass, it is a great opportunity to elevate others and ourselves.

A goal of this book is to guide the thoughtful wine drinker through this elevation. It is to make the most of these congenial pockets of order of the 12 drop rule and 12 drop experience in a world that may not have enough of them. As the columnist Maureen Dowd has said, "The flood of information overwhelms meaning." Perhaps slowing the flood and contemplating what the 12 drop rule and 12 drop experience can do is an opportunity to be seized so that flow, gratification, and wisdom connect in ways that build the better you. The British novelist Alexander McCall Smith in *A Conspiracy of Friends* is alluding to something parallel to the 12 drop experience when he has a character speak of risotto: "You can eat it very slowly, if you like, grain by grain, cherishing each one. That's how we should approach life, I think. We should savour every little bit of it, every single grain."

—⁓—

Savoring and mindfulness can be connected, and the opportunities are there in wine appreciation and conversation. While meditation and mindfulness seem to be considered for everything—from childrearing to human resource retreats to research labs—the possibilities are not exploited as they can be. There were more than four hundred scientific articles on mindfulness published in 2012 alone, for example. But mindfulness is not really everywhere, and there are possibilities to advance its practice and find new ways to augment it. Stress reduction appears to be the focus of much meditation and mindfulness, but it is desirable to find new ways of ritualizing meditation and mindfulness and finding somewhat different purposes for them.

Along with the attention to meditation and mindfulness, the recent growth of positive psychology and behavioral economics has brought increased interest in understanding and tweaking everyday activities to enhance possibilities to thrive. This new focus has launched dozens of fresh areas for research on topics that are directly accessible to the attentive public in ways that lead to self-improvement and rekindle older philosophical traditions. Happiness and wisdom are now fashionable again, opening up a variety of creative ways for individuals to renew the pursuit of the good life.

This book is about establishing techniques of assembling and clarifying your practical wisdoms and attaching these to the rituals of enjoyment of wine—in this case, the last dozen drops of wine in a bottle. Getting the "flow" right, both of wine and practical wisdoms, is what drives this book. This generates a new kind of mindfulness in a world where the pressures and velocities of living make it difficult to find moments to engage in meaningful contemplation.

Practical wisdoms can be defined as simply stated perspectives and strategies that shape a disposition so that a person can enjoy greater effectiveness in life and be more responsive to life's challenges. They are about finding an internal balance of effectiveness and responsiveness that works for the individual but also has positive consequences for society. Einstein said, "Life is preparation for the future." Cultivation of a positive disposition toward the future is the nurturing of what the Canadian author and Harvard professor Michael Ignatieff alludes to as "a shrewd humility," and practical wisdoms can be central to that process.

Effectiveness means acting with clarity and focus toward a goal without unnecessarily damaging another of your goals. Responsiveness is attending to the needs of others and the requirements of a situation. It is the consummate practical wisdom when one can design a combination of effectiveness and responsiveness that has the highest quality possible for an individual and expresses the individuality of that person. There is shrewdness in this that is both satisfying and forward-looking.

The late English philosopher Michael Oakeshott said that it is not easy to do this because technical knowledge is fairly easy to transmit but practical knowledge is not. *New York Times* columnist David Brooks adds that there are reservoirs of practical wisdoms out there that can be tapped but often are not. The spirit of modern democracies makes it hard to dip into these reservoirs as younger and "fresher" leadership seems to be more valued. Rapid processes of change seem simultaneously to depreciate wisdoms but also substantiate a need to replenish them. This quandary needs to be addressed in a variety of ways.

This book takes on this task in a playful but disciplined manner. Tapping the reservoirs of practical wisdoms is both easy and difficult. It is easy in that civilizations accumulate them; it is difficult in that choosing among them and implementing them as individuals prove challenging. This task is not as daunting as one might think, however. Practical wisdoms are not that complex—they are normally elegant, representing an ease of access and an economy of presentation. But settling on which ones you will embrace and incorporating them into a philosophy of living are challenging. One usually needs more than one mechanism to accomplish this; as we will see in the next chapter, using the 12 drop rule and 12 drop experience is one way to begin.

Practical wisdoms seem to proliferate, whether from folklore—"A stitch in time saves nine"—or from the latest self-help books on leadership. Some of the strongest practical wisdoms are reflected and reinforced in religious or philosophical terms; the easiest example is the Golden Rule: Do unto others as you wish them to do unto you. It is a marvelous statement of the value of reciprocity even if it does not tell you what others really wish for you to do. As a practical wisdom, it has attractiveness; but I will argue in chapter 4 why it did not make my personal list of top twelve practical wisdoms.

Practical wisdoms may be elegant, but they still require thinking through. John F. Kennedy famously said, "Too often we...enjoy the comfort of opinion without the discomfort of thought." The search for meaning and practical wisdoms has many a curve, but the search is worth it as a process and because it can lead to fortuitous conclusions. This book promotes the search and helps navigate the curves.

Practical wisdoms are not as easy to compile as a grocery list; they emerge and thrive only with concentration, skill, conversation, and practice. And they are often more complex than their brevity suggests. Despite this, creating such a list is an achievable quest and one that ought to command our attention. The reward is an individualized set of practical wisdoms that contributes to a higher sense of personal efficacy.

There are thousands of practical wisdoms that emerge from religious traditions, folklore, philosophies, and myths. Whether these create practical wisdoms or simply reflect and refine them can be debated. Individuals tap from this huge array in their journeys through life. The argument of this book is that an internal balance of effectiveness and responsiveness—your sense of personal efficacy—is sustained by a relatively small set of practical wisdoms that invigorates a person and expresses a philosophy of living. Readers are invited to explore the world of practical wisdoms and choose those that that can guide your life. This book is a stimulus to that search, but every search is unique.

There is virtue in clarifying these practical wisdoms and bringing them to a fuller consciousness. Many possible techniques exist to accomplish this, and this book promotes a playful way to do it by blending wine appreciation and a disciplined mindfulness. There are fascinating books, such as *Wine and Philosophy: A Symposium on Thinking and Drinking*, edited by Fritz Allhoff, that usefully explore the serious issues associated with philosophy, art, and wine talk. And there are works, like *The*

Accidental Connoisseur, that delightfully combine wine appreciation, philosophizing, and travelogue. Roger Scruton's *I Drink Therefore I Am* was especially influential for me in that he spoke about "a chain of linked symposia, in which the catalyst is wine, the means conversation, the goal a serene acceptance of our lot and a determination not to outstay our welcome." I have taken Scruton's observation and converted it to a new cottabus, thus validating not only him but also all those who have linked wine and philosophizing in the thousands of years since humans created the elixir of the gods.

The opportunity I seized upon is a down-to-earth, regular way to tease out an individual's philosophy of living in the rituals of enjoyment of wine; it takes the seemingly simple exercise of watching the last drops of wine drain from a bottle as both a metaphor and a platform—a metaphor for the next chunks of a person's life and a platform for methodically outlining the pursuit of the practical wisdoms that define one's philosophy of living

I refer to a philosophy of living rather than a philosophy of life because the former tends to be more dynamic and forward-looking than the latter. A philosophy of living requires practical wisdoms to make life happen well and to anticipate change, whereas a philosophy of life often seems reflective, retrospective, and general—perhaps even static. Most people, social scientists tell us, underestimate the possibilities for change in their lives. A philosophy of living corrects for this and has solid roots in an Epicurean attentiveness to living as opposed to a preoccupation with death and a possible afterlife. Einstein agreed when he said that "the best preparation for the future is to live as if there were none." For Epicurus, virtue and pleasure were interdependent. His approach can be visualized as a triangle with the base as a philosophy of living and two other sides: pleasure and happiness. Pleasure, for Epicurus, was based in positive sensations and varied in duration, and it reached its maximum limit with the mitigation of pain.

Epicurus taught that happiness depends on foresight and agreeable friendships in a society where one has no fear of others and where one can cultivate wisdom. This finishes a triangle of a philosophy of living, pleasure, and happiness. Epicurus had other concerns, too, especially in the study of nature and the elaboration of the atomic theory of Democritus. But it is the triangle of a philosophy of living, pleasure, and happiness that animates this book, circumscribing the practical wisdoms that fill the triangle and nurture the authentic connections of the three sides.

An Epicurean philosophy of living is not usually understood well in American popular culture that seems to see it as a strenuous love of fine food and wine. On the contrary, Epicurus had a simple formula for living: 1) Do not fear the gods or death; and 2) Good things are easy to obtain and evils are easy to endure. This formula was driven by prudence and definitely not by the excesses of pleasure. In his letter to Menoeceus, Epicurus states, "And since pleasure is our first and native good, for that reason we do not choose every pleasure whatsoever, but will often pass over many pleasures when a greater annoyance ensues from them." He goes on to say, "And often we consider pains superior to pleasures when submission to the pains for a long time brings us as a consequence a greater pleasure." Later in the same letter, Epicurus says, "By pleasure we mean the absence of pain in the body and trouble in the soul. It is not an unbroken succession of drinking bouts and of revelry, not sexual lust, not the enjoyment of fish and other delicacies of a luxurious table, which produce a pleasant life; it is sober reasoning, searching out the grounds of every choice and avoidance, and banishing the beliefs through which the greatest tumults take possession of the soul."

Finding the real Epicurus and getting him to work for our happiness are goals for this book. As you will see, Epicurus's thought still resonates among modern thinkers including psychologists, sociologists, economists, and organizational theorists. The rediscovery of Epicurus in the early 1400s was one of the keys to the flourishing of science and reason in the Renaissance and Enlightenment, greatly influencing generations of intellectual and political leaders including Thomas Jefferson. One could even argue that only Machiavelli's writing, a century after the rediscovery of Epicurus, had as much influence on the emerging modern senses of self and personal efficacy. Epicurus's continued relevance speaks to not only the durability of his thinking, but also the hunger to find satisfying philosophies of living in today's fast-paced world.

Epicurus lived in the times of the collapse of Alexander's empire and at a point in Greek history when philosophical thought flourished, as can be seen in his contemporaries, Plato and Aristotle. Epicurus's thinking was distinguished from that of other major philosophers by his positive juxtaposition of pleasure, happiness, and the good. He further distinguished himself in emphasizing wisdom over philosophy itself. In his letter to Menoeceus, Epicurus states: "Wisdom is a more precious thing even than philosophy." And wisdom is often difficult to find, particularly in the hypervelocity of social media in the modern world. One needs to slow down the tempo of life in order to get the pacing right. The 12 drop rule is one of many possibilities to slow the pace of life, but it is perhaps the most pleasurable.

A proper sense of Epicurus is necessary to apprehend the possibilities of the 12 drop rule and the 12 drop experience. This chapter has established the 12 drop rule and an historical precedent, the ancient game of cottabus that used the last drops of wine in a vessel as part of philosophical discussions. It is consistent with Epicurus's attention to nature as he saw that the study of nature as helping one to discern the limits of things. And, of course, there are limits to the number of drops in a bottle of wine. Chapter 2 elaborates the 12 drop rule into the 12 drop experience that encourages mindfulness and conversation. It spells out the new cottabus that will help individuals collect and refine a set of practical wisdoms that advances their happiness. Chapter 3 probes more extensively Epicurean teachings in an imagined conversation between Epicurus and one of his most famous followers, Thomas Jefferson. Chapter 4 is autobiographical, describing my search for practical wisdoms as an example of how to configure a set of wisdoms that expresses a vision of who you are and that flows with some logic. And chapter 5 guides you through using the last drops of wine to think through your practical wisdoms so as to remember them; articulating your set of practical wisdoms establishes your "personal terroir" or landscape and can be reinforced in the context of a sacred geography—a wine region that has compelling qualities for you. In my case this is the Monticello appellation of Virginia.

—⁂—

The 12 drop rule is ultimately about flow—less about the physics of it (which I do set out in Appendix A) and more about the psychological-existential flow that many positive psychologists analyze and celebrate. One of the founders of positive psychology, Mihaly Csikszentmihalyi, made the study of flow central to his approach. He researched the memory of happiness in people and found that pleasure alone could not explain it, particularly since it is hard to sustain pleasure over any extended period of time. He discovered that it is flow—a sense of being in a zone of virtually effortless and productive movement—that people remember and try to re-create. That sense that "everything is going right" can be sensational in the broadest sense of the term.

Watching the last twelve drops is more than the pleasures of enjoying the wine and companionship; it is what psychologist Martin Seligman refers to as "gratifications" that fully engage one's strengths and place one in an exciting and memorable experience. Jonathan Haidt, a University of Virginia psychologist, speaks of the skepticism felt by many regarding hedonistic pleasures, but also their awe at what "extends" our strengths and prolongs them. When Epicurus spoke of pleasure, he really was speaking of gratifications, in my view. Epicurus's pleasures do not speak of hedonistic excess but of prudence, friendship, pursuit of wisdom, and zones of tranquility that celebrate the strengths of life—in other words, gratifications.

The flow of this book is about nurturing gratifications—gratifications which themselves flow from the 12 drop experience, the elucidation of practical wisdoms, and the discovery of sacred geographies that bring out the best in us. So let's see where the flow now takes us in the 12 drop experience.

CHAPTER 2

THE 12 DROP EXPERIENCE

What is the 12 drop experience? It begins with the enjoyment of a glass of wine and the realization that the bottle will soon be empty. Instead of seeing this as a problem to be simply solved by opening another, the 12 drop rule instigates an opportunity to add something new—a new wine ritual that complements the rituals associated with anticipating and enjoying the first drops of wine in a bottle. We have rituals of smelling and tasting that have become part of the wine experience and have become highly stylized, so much so that we tease wine "snobs" and wine "geeks" about their often subjective reporting of a wine experience. This book is about the last drops of wine in a bottle and the shaping of a new wine ritual—a new cottabus. This new cottabus is about pursuit of practical wisdoms, happiness, and a sociability that mimics the elegance of the toast but places it in a larger discussion of a philosophy of living.

A new scholarly movement, anticipated by nineteenth-century utilitarians and called the "science of happiness," explores methodically the components of happiness. Our new cottabus complements that by establishing a method, based on scientific principles (the 12 drop rule), that grows into sustained reflection and an orderly shaping of a set of practical wisdoms that begin to establish an individual's pursuit of happiness. And the truth of the 12 drop rule is objective—even more objective than points granted to wines by Robert Parker (even as I admit his considerable skill as wine guru). The science of the 12 drop rule may not be as relevant to happiness as the science of winemaking is to the making of fine wines. But the 12 drop rule is about a study of nature that gives shape and direction to wine appreciation by providing a new dimension to it, specifically a philosophically minded exercise that pursues truth as much like art as science.

This book has two central characters: Epicurus and Thomas Jefferson. As we will see more fully in chapter 3, Epicurus and Jefferson made a study of nature central to their thinking. Combining science and philosophy was relatively easy for both of them, although there could be discomfort and delay in moving from thought to action. For Jefferson, in particular, the discomfort came in many forms. Science and knowledge, for Jefferson, came in small increments. Jefferson certainly found frustration in trying to grow wine grapes in Virginia. And no doubt he would have been disappointed that it would take so long for American winemaking to take off. He would have been angry at the huge error of Prohibition, of course. Like Epicurus, he would have been delighted by the growth of the science of winemaking in the late twentieth century. The study of nature has accelerated in almost every arena, and universities from UC Davis to Virginia Tech excel in advancing the science of winemaking. Jefferson knew of the power of universities, given his commitment to the formation of the University of Virginia. And Jefferson's fascination with agriculture and agricultural improvement certainly shaped the great land-grant university system in the nineteenth century that eventually led to the UC Davis powerhouse. These developments would have heartened both Epicurus and Jefferson.

But it is not only the study of nature that advances truth and progress. Epicurus would have argued that a robust introspection of one's own life was essential. In the thinking of both Epicurus and Jefferson, science *and* philosophy were required to advance truth, and the effort also had to be artful. There is a bit of science in the 12 drop rule—observation, recording of facts, and explanation of why there is always a minimum of twelve drops left after normal pouring. But the truth this book explores is the robust introspection and articulation about life that is similar to philosophy and art. The French novelist and philosopher Muriel Barbery says art "'gives shape' to our emotions, makes them visible and, in so doing, places a seal of eternity upon them." To adapt Wordsworth, the 12 drop rule is about "spots of time" that are savored and lift us up.

But is this not frivolous? Barbery again: "Those who feel inspired... by the greatness of small things will pursue them to the very heart of the inessential where, cloaked in everyday attire, this greatness will emerge from within a certain ordering of ordinary things and from the certainty that *all is as it should be*, the conviction that *it is fine this way*." As we will see shortly, Nietzsche speaks of how important it is to have "those who know how to make much of little." And noted author Alain de Botton stated: "To condemn ourselves for these minute concerns is to ignore how rich in meaning details may be."

What are we to do with these "spots of time" of the last drops? How should we engage in robust introspection? There are many devices to encourage mindfulness that come from religions, self-help movements, and various other sources. The 12 drop rule is one of those devices, discovered and named by my wife and me, that I propose to develop for those who are lovers of wine and are philosophically minded. The specific method was suggested by poet and critic Geoffrey O'Brien in an essay on silent movies in the *New York Review of Books* in May of 2012; he spoke of "watching" as a "kind of eavesdropping." Watching the last twelve drops is eavesdropping on the "spots of time" in a life or lives. It is listening to unarticulated and often unordered thoughts so as "to make much of little" and gain greater self-knowledge that can be shared with others. And it is about making these thoughts articulate and ordered.

Now it is time to more specifically define the 12 drop experience by identifying twelve (what else!) "spots of time" associated with it. The twelve below can be seen as stages that typically unfold chronologically. It is about taking the force of the 12 drop rule and socializing it. This is about art more than about science, but both are needed in the pursuit of truth.

—◠◡◠—

A Playful Pause as One Finishes a Bottle of Wine with Friends

What makes a pause playful? You and your friend or friends have just finished your first bottle of wine together, and the alcohol has already begun to lubricate conversation. There is a discussion about whether to open or order a second bottle (we all know the answer to this but go through the rhetorical motions to show others either how responsible we are or how much we are a party animal). After the almost inevitable decision to open a second bottle, the first has had a chance to consolidate those last drops for the 12 drop rule.

If your friends have not heard of the 12 drop rule, you challenge them by declaring the rule and begin to measure the number of drops as they fall. At first the drops come quickly, making it difficult to count, with perhaps contentious claims about how many there were in the first seconds. By the time the last six or so come out, velocity is slower and there is ease at counting and anticipating the twelfth drop. Debates about how many drops have fallen are usually extinguished early on as normally more than twelve drops are in evidence. Almost inevitably someone will think of all this as a silly party trick. You are now left with a decision: Do you simply admit this and move onto something else, or do you begin a conversation about how to give more meaning to this playful pause? If you decide the former, it affirms a trivial playfulness; if you decide the latter, you must find triggers that encourage the playful search for meaning to continue. Just as in a board game, there have to be directions, but the players construct the directions as the exercise continues. And continue it shall if you shape it correctly in the beginning and return to it as bottles of wine are consumed over time and at other occasions.

What conversational triggers are there? We know people like lists—as in favorite movies, books, restaurants, or vacation spots. Why not launch the 12 drop experience by beginning to produce a list of practical wisdoms that define what you are about?

But why practical wisdoms rather than something else? Barry Schwartz and Kenneth Sharpe, authors of the 2010 book *Practical Wisdom*, state that human societies need rules and principles but that practical wisdom is needed to apply them well in specific circumstances that require moral and emotional sensibilities. They assert the need for both empathy and "moral improvisation" as we balance and bend rules. Just as we need books, movies, and vacations to flourish in the modern world, we need practical wisdoms to creatively pursue happiness and negotiate the journey of life. According to Schwartz and Sharpe, these are "hard-earned skills." Lists of these wisdoms are more difficult to develop than other lists and need to be refined and communicated to others. Philosophical symposia can help with this, and the ancient Greeks and Romans had fun with it around the cottabus game. Our new cottabus renews the connection between wine and philosophy as we use the 12 drop experience to shape mini-symposia on practical wisdoms and the pursuit of happiness.

These mini-symposia rarely can be completed in one sitting or on one occasion because sustained reflection and the making of a practical wisdom diary are required to keep track of your personal search for such wisdoms. What at first seems to be a simple task becomes an evolution and refinement of ideas about who you are and how you present yourself to others. So conversational triggers emerge from your giving a couple of examples from your own list or from the body of maxims and wisdom statements that proliferate in every culture. This begins to establish a platform for continued discussion over time, even as it is interrupted by a change in the flow of conversation or by the conclusion of the social event itself.

Examples of practical wisdoms should come easily: "Do unto others as you would wish them to do unto you." "A stitch in time saves nine." "A penny saved is a penny earned." This is a precursor to a more sophisticated search process that has the goal of identifying the twelve practical wisdoms that personally define you. The second stage of the

12 drop experience speaks to what has to be overcome and helps explain why it will take several sessions.

—ɯ—

Finding the Balance of Seriousness and Frivolity and Dissolving the Difference

One of the ways to find balance between seriousness and frivolity is to conceive of the 12 drop experience as poetry. The Spanish philosopher Santayana alludes to the "things that have their poetry not because of what we make them symbols of, but because of their own movement and life." Seriousness can come not just by using the twelve drops as metaphor, but in the psychological moment when we are in "sympathy with the movement of things." And sympathy with nature is powerful, for Santayana, as a "poetry of nature may be discerned merely by the power of intuition which it awakens and the understanding it employs." Given this, the 12 drop rule and the 12 drop experience are rooted in a seriousness that appreciates movement and calls out for understanding of nature and ourselves.

At first blush, the 12 drop experience seems to err on the side of frivolity. But as it is taken to its conclusion, it probes areas of the psyche and one's character that can become very sensitive. After all, the 12 drop experience is about outlining a philosophy of living that is understandable to yourself and to your friends. It is more self-help than therapy. It works when it finds a balance between seriousness and frivolity, but it thrives when it dissolves the difference between the two. There are examples of success in doing this in the world of television. Neal Gabler, writing in the *New York Times* in May of 2013, reflected on the upcoming retirement of Barbara Walters. Ms. Walters, he said, was both entertainer and journalist and "erased the line between the serious and the frivolous," thus changing the television news industry to this day. Walters was criticized by many, of course, but the changes she instigated have stuck.

The 12 drop experience is neither a parlor game nor a substitute for therapy. It is consistent with the Buddhist principle of mindfulness—a reflective, relaxed, and quiet position that can produce wisdom and peace. Mindfulness can follow from technique and the creation of zones of tranquility. The playful pause of the 12 drop experience begins this process and cannot be completed quickly in the social occasion of wine appreciation. The 12 drop experience is to be shared, but it flourishes only if one does the homework of searching methodically for a set of practical wisdoms that is unique to you.

As we have seen, another way to conceptualize the 12 drop experience is to think of "watching" as "a kind of eavesdropping." Watching the drops fall is also about watching the other ponder and enjoy the experience. We all know the importance of body language in communication. How friends or even food servers begin to handle the 12 drop rule and 12 drop experience is often rich in observation. Montaigne says we should "observe, observe perpetually." Assessing the reactions of others is like spying—a testing of how the other balances seriousness and frivolity.

Wine appreciation almost always has the character of both seriousness and frivolity, so it is not a large leap to seeing the 12 drop experience that way. The "sweet spot" is finding a way to dissolve the difference. It is not hard given the nature of wine appreciation. The Sufi poet Rumi sees the result as "joy, a winelike freedom that dissolves the mind and restores the spirit." The real test of the 12 drop rule is to discover the capacity for not only enjoying wine and friendship, but also finding joy in deeper dialogues and self-reflections about who we are and strategizing about how we can explain ourselves to others.

—∞—

Knowing How to Make Much of Little...
—Nietzsche

This third stage of the 12 drop experience inaugurates the effort to find practical wisdoms in the commonplace of daily living. It is not only the poor who make much of little. During the Great Depression and in World War II the general population took pride in individual and collective efforts to stretch resources. Those habits continued for many after World War II, but the advent of prosperity and rising incomes often eroded the wisdom of stretching resources. Reactions against materialism and consumption-based living grew, however, not only in the environmental movement but also in disgust with waste, litter, and the epidemic of obesity. The 12 drop experience reminds us of traditions of saving, stretching resources, and prudent behaviors that exist within a social context. Self-help need not be an isolated or isolating experience—invoking a social dimension accelerates and supports individual improvement. Proliferation of support groups and the growth of life coaching both give testimony to the social and cultural dimensions of desirable habits.

But getting much of little is not simply about getting an extra sip or two from a bottle of wine. And it is more than generating a playful conversation with a friend. It is about establishing a platform for methodically articulating a philosophy of living around practical wisdoms. This gets much, much more from the bottle of wine.

The 12 drop experience is more than a methodology, of course. It is a lever for creativity that uses curiosity about character to give shape to something real yet new—a structure and configuration of practical wisdoms that express the artistry and poetry of your individual identity and character. Like any good work of art, it should elevate and transport you to fresh and promising regions. And it is not static. Just as artists often play with the same theme and generate new variations of their work, so can you generate variation by adding practical wisdoms and maxims as they become compelling to you. There is a need to "discipline your canvas," however, by limiting the number of practical wisdoms that define you. Twelve is not a magic number (although some numerologists would insist that it is). Rather, for our purposes, it is a somewhat arbitrary standard that can guide you as you express the poetry of who you are.

The 12 drop experience encourages imagination, even if it is construed as an autobiographical exercise married to wine appreciation. The author and reporter Adam Gopnik similarly has spoken about a "historical imagination," stating, "It's simply the ability to see small and think big." Seeing the smallness of a drop of wine and using it to think big about who you are is at the heart of the 12 drop experience, thus making much of little. Now, onto the fourth stage of the 12 drop experience.

—⟋⟍—

Being Attentive to Details

The novelist Carmen Posadus writes: "People, like drops of wine, come in pieces, eye-catching details that sum up their personalities." Curiosity about character leads, almost inexorably, to establishing the practical wisdoms that begin to define a person. One's temperament also defines a person, and it is the attention to this detail that brings to real life an understanding of character. Character is built around commitments, while personality has fluidity to it—optimism and pessimism can fluctuate, as can self-confidence or a sense of personal efficacy. It is often details of personality that attract us to another, whether a personal warmth or a sparkle in the eyes. We often react positively to those who seem playful, and we respect those who display seriousness or empathy. We often react negatively to someone who is dour or self-centered even before we begin to know them better. These "pieces" begin to sum up another's personality as we experience them.

Experience and wisdom are related. The novelist Terry Pratchett states: "Wisdom comes from experience. Experience is often a result of a lack of wisdom." As personalities gather experience, so can wisdom grow—even though it is a complicated dance. The 12 drop experience is mostly about people, not wine. It is about generating a watchful attentiveness to two kinds of detail: the drops of wine themselves and the ways others react to the experience of the 12 drop rule. It is similar to watching how others react to a joke. If well told, there is appreciation, and if not well told, there can be a groan or a pitying laugh in response. Some react to the 12 drop rule by wondering why anyone would pay attention to the physics of it, while others want to know the story or significance of the exercise. A smile evoked by the first experience of the 12 drop rule often begins to sum up the personality of the other, whether that is playfulness, optimism, or condescension. Counting drops and watching the other are, together, a creative moment in which you can learn more about the other and whether that person has a capacity to probe the significance and potential meanings of the experience.

The easiest way to probe its significance is to use the 12 drop rule as a metaphor for life and the biological reality of its emptying in death. Like life, the last drops of wine come with some sadness that there may be only a little more we can squeeze from it. There is promise in it, too, that somehow we can slow the velocity of life so that we can hold it and reflect upon it.

—m—

Réjouir—the Thrill of Anticipating the Future

Using the metaphor of the 12 drop rule as a way to anticipate the end of life may be a fine way to begin probing the significance of the rule, but the 12 drop rule is more—and it needs to be. Following Montaigne's maxim to "observe, observe perpetually," a pillar of the 12 drop experience is the thrill of anticipating the future—what the French call *réjouir*. It is the anticipation of the last drops as we ascertain whether the twelve-drop minimum will be achieved and how many more drops will display themselves.

Excitement builds as the drops come more slowly; the thrill is in watching the slowing and wondering if the rule will be confirmed.

This seems to be the antithesis of the common experience of aging wherein the velocity of time seems to accelerate in what Jane Fonda calls the last third of life. There are many possible explanations for this; the most compelling to many, at least at first, is that each day represents a smaller fraction of one's total life. When one is young, each day seems to take forever. Réjouir, for the preadolescent and adolescent, seems to be in a distant future, and it seems to come much too slowly. The central beauty of the 12 drop experience is turning this commonplace on its head so that the perceived velocity of life slows dramatically in its last third. The thrill of awaiting the last drops in their maddening slowness becomes a spot of time for reflecting on life and getting the most of each day. We could even call this the "slow wine" movement, as a corollary to the slow food movement. Slow food has many virtues, as does slow wine.

There are important pleasures attached to slowing the velocity of both eating and wine drinking. According to author Jeff Gordinier, "Mindful eating…is about experiencing food more intensely—especially the pleasures of it." Of course, sipping wine during a meal slows down the pace of eating and combines the pleasures of wine and food. The 12 drop experience reminds us of this advantage by bringing it to our consciousness. This reminder is necessary because mindful eating and mindful drinking are difficult to do, especially for Americans. The 12 drop experience forces a pause in the normal pacing of dinner so that the matter of mindfulness can be better addressed.

There are many devices to help one slow the velocity of time. The popularity of yoga and tai chi resonates also with the continuing tide of Buddhist practices of meditation and mindfulness, for example. The 12 drop experience complements these devices and techniques in a small ritual as one finishes a bottle of wine with friends. It is a robust reminder that slowing the velocity of life is possible—that although the physical world is inexorable, there are ways to temper its inexorability with a physics that postpones conclusions.

But the psychological question, which Epicurus would have loved, is whether the sense of the increasing velocity of time with aging is real or urban myth. Richard A. Friedman, a professor of clinical psychology and the director of the psychopharmacological clinic at the Weill Cornell Medical College, believes it to be real, and he attributes it to the steeper learning curves of the young. He states, "Most adults do not explore and learn about the world the way they did when they were young; adult life lacks the constant discovery and endless novelty of childhood." His remedy for the perceived faster velocity of time as one grows older is to continue learning. Having a plan for doing so is crucial and is a key practical wisdom.

This practical wisdom is more difficult to put into effect than it seems. An article in *Science* in January of 2013 spoke of the "end of history illusion." Psychologists found that most people "underestimate how much they will change in the future." Imagining change is more difficult than remembering how you have changed in the past. The thrill of anticipating the future needs to be nurtured frequently, not just at commencement and wedding ceremonies. That is why réjouir is so central to the 12 drop experience.

As we will see with Epicurus and even Jefferson, the thrill of anticipating the future need not be driven by a belief in an individualized afterlife. Epicurus argued vigorously against individual immortality, and Jefferson—although believing in an afterlife—was very Epicurean in getting the most out of life itself. The advent of earthly happiness and its celebration, according to Santayana, occurred with Lucretius's poem "On the Nature of Things" in 57 BC in testimony to the power of Epicurus's thought. Santayana says of Lucretius and Epicurus that they held that "nothing arises in this world not helped to life by the death of some other thing." One need not believe in reincarnation to believe that the cycles of life are thrilling; make most of the life you have—and keep learning. Now on to the sixth stage of the 12 drop experience.

—ɯ—

A Celebration of Both Nature and the Human Capacity for Discovery and Inventiveness

While mindful eating and drinking may seem like a withdrawal from the social landscape of a meal into individual meditation, the 12 drop experience must walk on two legs, both meditative and social. In a cycle of reflection and celebration, each reinforces the other, and we are invited to forge new patterns of learning and expression. Once the first enjoyments of finding the 12 drop rule occur, its repetition becomes a call to ritual to review the status of your reflections and how you are beginning to decide the practical wisdoms that define you. It's as if you are watching yourself in the company of others; and this watching is celebratory.

What is celebrated is, first, a gift of nature because fermentation of grapes is a natural phenomenon discovered by humans and, through invention, shaped into a myriad of refinements. The inventiveness has to do with more than wine; it is about all the devices, mechanical and cultural, involved in its making; about how to do fermentation well over a variety of conditions and how to adapt wine appreciation in a variety of cultural environments. What are developed are not only techniques of fermentation, but also modes of transport, finance, marketing, and diffusion of best practices in a competitive but cooperative environment. Also invented are cultural uses—whether toasting, cottabus, or simply sealing a deal. Wine publications today celebrate not only the number of points assigned to wines, but the personalities and leadership associated with the promotion of the wine industry.

The celebrations embedded in the 12 drop experience are, however, a very particular manifestation that is unique to those involved in learning the 12 drop rule and preparing to use it as a platform for articulating their own wisdoms. But what if your discoveries are too meager or vague? The answer is in persistence—or, perhaps better, in inventing practical wisdoms that capture your creative spirit and uniqueness. For most of us, though, uniqueness displays itself in the configuration of practical wisdoms chosen and not in a given practical wisdom. It is unlikely that any two people will have the same set. There often will be much in common, however, and conversations may be compelling as we borrow and adapt from one another. There can be a dynamic quality to any individual's set of practical wisdoms; keeping a diary of candidates for your practical wisdoms is necessary so as to keep track of them, their sources, and the reasons you chose them or discarded them.

—◊◊◊—

A Specific Reminder that Winemaking Is Now a Science Based on Measurement

Although wine is often described as poetry or even as philosophy in a bottle, modern winemaking is now more science than art. Great universities like UC Davis and Virginia Tech not only pursue robust research programs but also help train the legions of professionals needed to support grape growing, fermentation, disease prevention, storage, and even marketing.

MIT scientist Erik Brynjolfson says, "The heart of science is measurement." And the management guru Peter Drucker has stated, "What's measured improves." The 12 drop rule is a measure that holds up to validation through repetition. It may not have the status that flows from a peer-reviewed academic article by a UC Davis researcher, but the 12 drop rule is fundamentally about measurement and is a catalyst to self-improvement. It is the utility of the 12 drop rule as a behavior-modifying tool when expressed as the twelve-drop experience that animates this book. Status and utility are what academics look for in their theories and models, but the layperson can find utility even when status is modest.

As science evolves, so too do social practices. This can be seen in the measurement of the seasons. While myth and superstition may have driven ancient calculation of solstices, the act of measurement led to predictive success and became surrounded by social practices such as rituals, parties, and celebrations that continue to this day. The rituals and social practices were inventions that often had resilience but sometimes did not. Only time will tell whether the 12 drop experience will have staying power.

It is possible that the 12 drop rule and the 12 drop experience will lead to other developments based on science and measurement. Lucretius's first-century BC poem in honor of Epicurus speaks to that possibility:

Thus time by degrees brings each several things forth before men's eyes and reason raises it up into the borders of light; for things must be brought to light one after another and in due order...until these have reached their highest point...

Who knows where the 12 drop rule and 12 drop experience will lead! Let's see where the eighth stage of the experience propels us.

—ɯ—

A Call to Ritual That Is Focused on Contemplation, Conversation, and Social Action

Confirming the 12 drop rule at a social occasion makes it a part of another ritual and shapes a variation in it. There is symmetry in the 12 drop rule in that a toast often occurs as a meal begins or at the first sips of wine. Confirming the 12 drop rule can lead to another toast as the meal ends or as a bottle of wine is finished. In some regions of Europe, getting the last drops of wine is considered a personal sign of good luck.

The 12 drop experience is asking for more, however; it is a call to mindfulness and further conversation about the struggles for self-improvement and happiness. The 12 drop experience becomes a ritual in and of itself because it has the stuff of ritual: the triggering mechanism, confirming the 12 drop rule, has the quality of invariance specified by anthropologists for ritual. Invariance refers to timeless repetition, in this case confirmation of the rule. The 12 drop experience itself becomes, as anthropologist Victor Turner would have it, a "social drama," a way of renewing oneself and small communities around the themes of the pursuit of happiness and practical wisdoms. In Jeffersonian terms, we struggle in the pursuit of happiness and find wisdom in the aftermath of experience. The 12 drop experience is a social drama that is a vessel of communication with others. It occurs around a powerful metaphor of the last drops of wine signifying the last parts of life. How does one confront the infirmities of aging and the knowledge that life, as we know it, is coming to an end? How do we find joy and wonder in it and not place all our eggs in the basket of an individual afterlife?

In sociological terms, the 12 drop experience is a code designed to encourage communication. In some ways it can be considered a "restricted" code—that is, one that is easily shared with family or friends. In other ways, it is becoming an "elaborated" code, one that is spelled out so that those who are unfamiliar with one another can find some clarity about the messages in the code. This book provides a model of communication about both the struggles for happiness and the delineation of practical wisdoms. It specifies procedures such as making notes and keeping a diary of the practical wisdoms that define our character and that potentially shape the broader social order. Even the rather arbitrary stipulation of twelve wisdoms conforms to ritual structure by formalizing an appropriate target number so that we pursue neither too few nor too many practical wisdoms. It is like a menu—too few items would not seem enough choice, whereas too many items may confuse or overwhelm us. The number twelve gives some basic sense of order to the communication. This is not an incipient ideology that may shape a broader social order; rather, it is a more dynamic and bottom-up process that lets the commitments of individual practical wisdoms construct more robust civic cultures that are responsive to the participants and encourage the sharing of those wisdoms. It is like a chorus that values both diversity and harmony, forcing us to listen to each other while fostering empathy.

The 12 drop experience is about more than mindfulness, then. It is about conversations leading to shaping a social order and increasing its radius of trust. By speaking of "practical" wisdoms we acknowledge wisdoms that have distinctly positive effects that can be easily shared with others. The sharing with others further increases the radius of trust as a virtuous circle; perhaps our politicians need new rituals like a new cottabus to help heal our paralyzed politics! The circle now turns to the ninth "spot of time" or stage in the 12 drop experience.

—⟊—

Looking to the Flow of Nature for Moral Inspiration

As we will see later when we examine Epicurus more carefully, there is in his work attention to nature as a source of wonder, metaphor, and inspiration. But Epicurus is not alone; indeed, looking to nature for inspiration is universal in cultures and is certainly not limited to the Romantic period of the nineteenth century. Almost any facet of nature can be used for inspiration; but when one sees movement in nature—whether of birth, seasons, tides, or streams—there is something there that also moves us. Poets often use flow as a metaphor; for example, Lucretius's poem in honor of Epicurus states, "No single things abide but all things flow. Fragment to fragment clings and thus they grow." The flow of wine can also move us.

The concept of flow is central to one of the most important scholars in the positive psychology movement, Mihaly Csikszentmihalyi. He suggests that people are at their happiest when in a state of flow—fully concentrated and absorbed in an experience. He speaks to a combination of skill and challenge in an experience—the personal skill being exercised to manage the experience and the challenge of the experience itself. While the 12 drop rule takes little skill to verify and is a relatively small challenge, the 12 drop experience requires a good deal of skill as a wisdom-seeker both to identify practical wisdoms and to regularly apply them.

Not only psychologists are attentive to flow. Alfred North Whitehead, the famed British philosopher, said that flow "is the first vague generalization which the unsystematized, barely analyzed, intuition of men has produced." He goes on to say, "The flux of things is one ultimate generalization around which we must weave our philosophical system." He refers to sense awareness and the experience of activity as "chunks in the life of nature." Epicurus would agree, and this author easily sees chunks as drops.

The 12 drop experience begins to give an identity to each of the last drops. And inspiration and experience conspire to make more of these identities. Change and permanence dance and leave us looking for new ways to adapt to the challenges of life. Practical wisdoms are devices each of use to accomplish this. The 12 drop experience leads us to a new kind of moral growth. Wordsworth might call the 12 drop experience—these "chunks in the life of nature"—"spots of time" that "retain a renovating virtue." It is a capacity to renew—that is, a way to bridge continuity and change in a way that inspires one to be better even when one falls short of expectation. The 12 drop rule and the 12 drop experience are opportunities to try again with a confidence in both the constancy of the rule and the promise of reconfirming our practical wisdoms, refining them and searching for new and more functional ones. Redemption is possible, even in secular terms.

Moral inspiration is within each of us as we reflect on experience and nature while attempting to figure out our better selves. We are not alone in this effort as we can tap the experience and distilled wisdom of others. The way we collect and configure our practical wisdoms establishes our uniqueness; but the practical wisdoms typically emerge from our culture and myths as Joseph Campbell has so eloquently argued. The wisdoms are rarely brand new, but that does not mean you have failed to put your stamp on them. Like most recipes, there is room for choice, emphasis, and substitution. If there were no room for growth, we would have only one old recipe book.

What is new is your own process of discovery of practical wisdoms. Your personal life experiences shape the discovery process. One rarely invents a new practical wisdom—what one invents are reformulated ones or ones that have been adopted from another culture. This is not trivial—it is creative inspiration when it occurs. And it is not a one-time occurrence—it should flow, first, as one begins to collect the practical wisdoms that you think guide you and, later, as you discover new ones that you can incorporate into your list. The secret is to make it a regular contemplation and find sources of inspiration in nature—and not just Google searches of wisdom sayings. And now to the important tenth stage of the 12 drop experience, so fundamental that it has inspired most of this book.

—◊◊◊—

Explaining and Describing Yourself

Jefferson said: "We ought not to die before we have explained ourselves to others." He especially was attentive to the demands and opportunities of living generations. Although believing in an afterlife, he was unwilling to rely on that future to resolve the issues and frustrations of life. The pursuit of happiness was anticipated by Epicurus but became foundational for Jefferson. And that pursuit had a moral core to it, an ought, of explaining oneself to others before we die. This moral core is the central opportunity of the 12 drop experience—finding an accessible way to do this by articulating the practical wisdoms that define us and becoming more explicit about them so as to be able to communicate them to others.

Scholars in the social sciences often specify four theoretical purposes: description, explanation, prediction, and planning. Description has a straightforward aim of reporting what is seen, what is perceived. Perceiving oneself is perhaps even harder, psychologists say. And explaining oneself to others adds another layer of difficulty. There are a variety of conventions for doing so that seem to combine or confuse description and explanation. People often use, for example, the categories of introversion or extroversion in this way. Or one says that men are from Mars and women from Venus. This approach privileges a perceived tendency and then finds a way to pragmatically ameliorate or balance it with features of the less dominant tendency.

Alternatively, we describe ourselves as a member of a culture. This may successfully establish an identity but not really explain oneself to another, given the problematic of stereotyping and the variety of individual characteristics. A specific configuration of practical wisdoms does support a more nuanced view of an individual along with a capacity for uniqueness. A person's set of practical wisdoms provides clues to life experiences, strategies of adaptation, and what we see as significant in a character. Others may share a given practical wisdom, but the collection of them has unique qualities that can explain much of yourself in a way that can be communicated with clarity. The search process itself will have a particular history, as will the massaging of the list as one reflects on and refines it.

As noted earlier, we frequently use lists to reveal ourselves in conversation. But these lists leave unanswered the question of what truly explains us and are more Trivial Pursuit than authentic explanations of ourselves to others. A set of practical wisdoms has much more possibility of revealing individual values, coping strategies, and what we perceive animates us. Establishing a set of practical wisdoms gives mindfulness a purpose and a focus. It centers the self without narcissism and avoids the nihilism of saying we can never really know ourselves or others.

The 12 drop experience is *not* about radically simplifying the process of explaining oneself to others. It is certainly not about the silliness of using an astrological sign to describe and explain oneself to another. And it is not about finding just one elegant or clever phrase, however useful, to accomplish this. Finding and refining a collection of practical wisdoms takes work, perhaps not as much as psychotherapy, but still an effort to make the list and continually review it. And the prospect of sharing it should be seen as a delicious opportunity to explain oneself to another before one dies. It may actually help people produce proper eulogies!

There is, then, embedded in the collection of practical wisdoms a sense of optimism and possibility—yes, even the possibility of happiness as the end is in sight. Thus we move to the eleventh stage of the 12 drop experience.

—∽—

Persistence and Patience Are Powerful Forces

The 12 drop experience leads one to privilege the twelfth drop over the first half dozen and even those that come after the twelfth. As those last few drops hang from the lip of the bottle, they seem to have a power over us—a power to force attention upon each of them. They seem to have an individuality lacking in the faster flow of the first half dozen drops. Life is like that, too; as one holds on, there is an understanding that persistence and patience are rewarded and that a life well led brings satisfaction and even joy. Judge Felix Frankfurter said it well: "Wisdom too often never comes, and so one ought not to reject it merely because it comes late."

As one tests the 12 drop rule over time, the practice generates serenity that confirms the regularity and predictability of life. As the cartoonist Charles Schultz has said: "I think I have discovered the secret of life. You just hang around until you just get used to it." There need not be profound searches for meaning or quests to confront angst. The accumulation of experience can produce a wisdom that is not particularly profound: Hanging around is good. The very slowness of the last drops focuses us on what we see and not the emptiness of the bottle after the last drop has fallen. What you see is what you get.

Focusing on the coming emptiness of a bottle and also of life can contribute to a complicated pessimism. In one of his novels, Reginald Hill has his hero groaning as he picks up a bottle of wine: "When he tipped it up, nothing came out. He peered inside with one eye and groaned again. It was deep and dark and empty as despair." Getting used to emptiness rarely leads to happiness, but getting used to life often does. Perhaps that is why many religions focus on an afterlife as a way to fill the emptiness. But would it not be better to get used to life and focus on what is real and perceptible?

The fear of death *is* real, even if it takes imagination to contrive to fill the emptiness after death. But the fear of death does not have to trigger the imagination, nor does it have to preoccupy us, even if we are believers. World renowned psychiatrist Norman Rosenthal says that "when the fear arises, I say to myself, 'It's a test that nobody fails. So you'll pass it too.' Accepting death lets you turn your attention to how you can defer the date and make best use of the time you have." And Peter Drucker could agree. "Time is the scarcest resource," he writes, "and unless it is managed nothing else can be managed."

Do nonbelievers have an advantage, then? They do not have to engage in the speculations, theory-building, and doctrinal exercises that can preoccupy the imaginations of believers. Most religions do find ways to be attentive to social justice and the demands of the living. There is little evidence that believers are more ethical than nonbelievers, however. Solace in the belief in an afterlife does not seem to produce more ethical behavior in the here and now. But neither does unbelief produce better behavior. The power of the last drops is not a monopoly of either those who believe in an afterlife or those who do not. Both experience life. It is for all who want to "hang around" and manage time as a scarce resource. But nonbelievers may have a small advantage for themselves as individuals: a laser-like focus on managing the rest of the time available to them, without being distracted by imagining the possibilities of a life after death. So thought Epicurus, and there may be a practical wisdom in that. That wisdom can also be a motivator. José Olazábal, captain of the European team in the 2012 Ryder Cup, rallied his golfers for a comeback win by saying, "All men die—not all men live." Death is a given, but a flourishing life is not.

But there must be advantages associated with belief and piety. A June 2013 article in *Social Science & Personality Science* found that pious believers were more likely to be content than nonbelievers. Other research has found believers to be more optimistic and healthier than nonbelievers. The research on happiness is more divided, however. The positive side of religion is often noticed by even those who are most skeptical (if not humorist Bill Maher!). Even Epicurus and Jefferson displayed piety, although with a healthy dose of anticlericalism.

The last stage of the 12 drop experience takes on the task of looking metaphorically at the emptying of the bottle.

—⟶⟵—

A Reminder That All Good Things Come to an End

The ancient Greeks were preoccupied with the nurturing and sustaining of the good life. But they embraced the mortality of humans as a "complement" to the immortality of the gods, according to Santayana. Even if one believes in individual human immortality, it does not necessarily have to diminish the sense that a good life is possible and desirable before one passes into a different dimension or a reincarnation. Science privileges the empirical over the metaphysical, but that does not mean reconciliation with religious doctrine and beliefs is impossible. Whitehead believed that a "philosophy of organism" could "heal the divided conscience of mankind and reconcile scientific thought with our religions and esthetic intuitions." The 12 drop experience need not, then, be a battleground between science and religion. It can be a sanctuary where that battle is avoided. It is a reminder that certain good things, including a fine bottle of wine, do come to their ends. Yet a new bottle of wine can be found, reproduction of life can occur, and posterity honored. This flexibility continues in the afterlife in many religions whose doctrines say that good behavior on earth leads to a heaven or desirable reincarnation and that bad behavior leads to a hell or lowly reincarnation.

Using common sense and science, one knows that drop number twelve is not the end of what is in the bottle. There are frequently more drops, and of course there are molecules and atoms that persist longer. While the experience comes to an end, there probably is not finality. Scientists tell us that atoms and subatomic particles are ubiquitous and rearrange themselves. The Harvard astronomer Harlow Shapley said, "We organic beings who call ourselves humans are made of the same stuff as the stars." Epicurus and the ancient Greek atomists said much the same thing, leaving ample room to be amazed by the wonders of nature.

We do need to place a limit on the 12 drop experience because waiting and waiting for the very, very last drop is dysfunctional. The management guru Jim Collins has said, "A great piece of art is composed not just of what is in the final piece, but equally important, what is not." The 12 drop experience is like a work of art because of what it includes but also what it does not include—perhaps a few more drops, a few more possible experiences. There were at least a dozen candidates for inclusion on the list of stages for the 12 drop experience that were not ultimately chosen because they could not contribute well to the flow of the 12 drop experience or were insufficient triggers to induce fruitful discussions for our mini-symposia, our new cottabus, our search for practical wisdoms.

Settling on twelve drops, twelve stages, and twelve practical wisdoms is not a static thing, nor is it a contraction of ambition. It is simply declaring an end when we all know that atoms and life somehow go on. The philosopher Clancy Martin has said that "life seems to get much of its meaning from the fact that it ends." We need to search for the meaning of our lives as we live them and as we manage our time, not after our lives. That does not mean losing ambition; a Kansas farmer, speaking of the need to reestablish a polyculture of vegetation on the high plains, said, "If you think you're going to complete your life's vision in your lifetime, you're not thinking big enough." It is good to manage your remaining time, but it is also good to have a big vision. Processes of change are afoot, and it is because good things—like life —come to an end. A new chapter beckons us.

CHAPTER 3

SOURCES OF PRACTICAL WISDOM: EPICURUS AND JEFFERSON

We have already seen glimpses of Epicurus and Jefferson in the previous chapter. It is now time to probe further. But why Epicurus and Jefferson when there are so many sources of practical wisdom from our own experience all the way from philosophically minded individuals from ancient Chinese, Persian, and Indian cultures to current songwriters, poets, and life coaches? There are five biographical reasons. First, Epicurus and Jefferson are both associated with the pleasures of wine (although Jefferson's affinity for the promotion and enjoyment of wine is much better documented than Epicurus's). Second, Jefferson was a self-proclaimed follower of Epicurus. Third, both have philosophical credentials, and both explicitly pursued practical wisdoms. Fourth, both have sympathy with the movement of things. And, fifth, both are materialists.

The last two reasons deserve some elaboration. Epicurus's philosophy, like that of many of the ancient Greeks, posited atoms in motion. Lucretius's poem in honor of Epicurus eloquently spoke to this: "No single things abide but all things flow. Fragment to fragment clings and thus they grow until we know them by name. Then by degrees they change and are no more the things we know." Epicurus was not fatalistic about change—he believed, as Stephen Greenblatt has written, in a "swerve" that could twist the inexorable dropping of atoms and initiate change or at least variation. In many ways Epicurus anticipated both

Hegel and Darwin—Hegel's positing of how quantitative and qualitative changes are mutually transformative, and Darwin's "frozen accidents" that characterize the paths of evolution.

Jefferson's sympathy with the movement of things had at least two features: his assiduous recordkeeping of nature and its changes and his notion of political change ("When in the course of human events..."). What Epicurus and Jefferson had in common to support their sympathy with the movement of things was the fifth reason for choosing them: their materialism. Epicurus denounced nonmaterial, mystical descriptions or explanations of nature. He followed the Greek school of thought that all was reduced to atoms. While it is not as clear whether Jefferson embraced ancient Greek atomic theory, he was certainly hostile to immaterial notions. In a letter to John Adams, he stated that to "talk of immaterial existences is to talk of nothings." Jefferson even referred in other writings to the "heresy of immaterialism" and accused those in the Christian tradition of a "masked atheism" for believing in immaterial beings.

Why is all this important for the 12 drop experience? Epicurus and Jefferson denied neither spirit nor piety, although their piety may appear superficial to most believers. Their attitude was to affirm life and the pursuit of wisdom and happiness and not look to a personal afterlife for answers. They thought it was idiotic to deny death, and, for each of them, looking to a personal afterlife to resolve matters of the present was unrealistic. They were concerned with the future in the sense that amplification of life should be a focus of the current generation, and such amplifications could also inform posterity. Reason, friendship, and wisdom were not simply goals for Epicurus and Jefferson but commitments, and commitments were practical wisdoms meant to focus an individual and give that person character and definition. Anticipating the future through these commitments further amplified life, whereas imagining an immaterial world and personal immortality diminished these commitments and seduced one to enter a world of illusion.

I find Epicurus's and Jefferson's approaches to the last drops of life appealing because they speak to a calculus that applies reason and realism to valuing what remains to individual biological life. One can be pious, as both Epicurus and Jefferson were, and still be compelled to make the most of life. Like Jefferson, one could believe in an afterlife without relying on it to inform the present. But why does this sound strange to many? Because we wonder why anyone would be pious if he was neither a deep believer in an afterlife nor convinced that Jesus's or the prophets' messages were transformational of individual lives. But researchers tell us that piety is useful for attachment to community, to health, and, yes, to happiness. Epicurus and Jefferson may not have had the sociological research to support this, but their sensibilities certainly picked up on it. Cultivating the 12 drop experience is about nurturing these same sensibilities. The bigger question is whether, as literary critic Barton Swain might argue, an Epicurean message could ever be as compelling as Jesus's or perhaps any other major religion's. But even if the answer is no, could the Epicurean message be a proper complement to even believers?

—☙—

There is also one autobiographical reason for choosing Epicurus and Jefferson, which flows from my time as a graduate student at the University of Virginia—Mr. Jefferson's university, as we students were taught to say in reverence to his vision at its founding. Jefferson placed the founding of the university on his tombstone as one of his three finest achievements. My graduate student experience served me well when I assumed an academic position in San Diego, where attention to wine is as prevalent as following the movie industry. The University of Virginia continues to hold great emotional power for me; my wife and I lived there when we were first married, and the beauty of the region was romantic (this was before the slogan "Virginia is for lovers"). There were other influences of the university, including its well-known honor system. It continued to bring out the best of me as my career blossomed in academic administration and as I did considerable research on academic integrity policies in American higher education, even receiving a lifetime achievement award in 2006 from the International Center for Academic Integrity.

So, the pull of Charlottesville is massive. And when my wife and I discovered the 12 drop rule, it just seemed natural to combine our love of wine with reminiscences of Mr. Jefferson's university and our delightful times there. It was a real plus especially as we followed the robust growth of the Virginia wine industry, virtually nonexistent when I was a graduate student in the 1960s but now counting more than two dozen wineries within twenty miles of Monticello and Charlottesville.

—ᴍ—

So how do we bring Epicurus and Jefferson to bear as sources of practical wisdoms that help us to define a self? One device, made famous by Dostoevsky's Grand Inquisitor scene in *The Brothers Karamazov*, is to imagine a conversation between Epicurus and Jefferson which can tease out possibilities just as Dostoevsky's imagined poetic "conversation" between the Grand Inquisitor and Jesus. The imagined give-and-take below will not likely rise to the literary stature of a Dostoevsky, but it begins to show a process that can move the 12 drop experience toward the goal of setting the personal practical wisdoms that define us. Without the specificity of commitment of practical wisdoms, there can be only an illusory self or a world of rigid religious beliefs. We need something in between—what the commentator Ross Douthat calls a "spiritual world" where principles and rules exist but there is flexibility in adapting them to the processes of change we encounter, helpful when principles are contradictory in a given situation. We used to call this situation ethics, but a spiritual world requires more principles than flexibility. Practical wisdoms can be what center us among principles, rules, and situation ethics. A given set of practical wisdoms held by an individual defines the individual as unique, thus guaranteeing that the self is not illusory.

Most of our practical wisdoms and our moral code come from theological sources, family, or orientation to the culture of an organizational world of corporate life. But establishing practical wisdoms is also a journey shaped by friendships and philosophically minded mentors, and these mentors often exist in our world of work. For example, the *New York Times* runs a fascinating series in its Sunday Business section built on interviews of CEOs to gauge what shaped them and how they see themselves as leaders and mentors. The series is filled with practical wisdoms that take the principles of production, profit, efficiency, and market share and shape them with a clarity that establishes what religious orders used to call the charism of a given order. *Integrity* is often a key word in these interviews, thus overcoming the improvisational flexibility that can characterize some individual or organizational behavior.

Epicurus and Jefferson would no doubt have identified friendship and reason as vitally important to them as mentors. And to have reasoned conversations with friends not only would bring them special joy but also would lead to sustained pursuits of practical wisdoms. We often need midwives in our efforts to articulate practical wisdoms; Epicurus and Jefferson are mine. Below, their fanciful conversation.

—⟋𝕎⟍—

Imagine: It is a fine April dawn in today's world, with the dogwoods in bloom as Epicurus joins Jefferson for a walk in the gardens of Monticello. Both were deeply attached to gardens: Epicurus's school was called the Garden, and Jefferson's love of nature has been well documented and celebrated, most notably by former Director of Gardens and Grounds and Gardens at Monticello, Peter Hatch. The ghosts of Epicurus and Jefferson could not but enjoy the beauty of the Monticello grounds as they walked about.

Jefferson speaks first: "Welcome to my gardens. You know that I am a confirmed follower of you. Your quotes inspired many others and me over the centuries—and still do. Ironically, neither of us had strong beliefs in an afterlife—and you even disbelieved in it—and yet we find ourselves here in conversation. Your thoughts have held up through the ages. Why do you think this has happened?"

Epicurus responds: "It almost did not. Lucretius's poem about me in 57 BC kept themes together, but many of my teachings were lost in the rise of Rome, the Stoic school of thought, and the disparagement of my teachings in the early Christian church. I was insufficiently fatalistic for the Stoics, and the Christians were very dissatisfied with my materialism and my skepticism about life after death and providential gods. The Christians could have noticed that we Greeks were pious in our own way, wanted companionship with the gods, and felt vicariously their powers. But humans are not gods because we cannot share their immortality. The Christians wanted it all, however, from the deification of Jesus to life everlasting for his followers.

"The Stoics seemed more influential in Rome than was I, and they could more easily connect with Christian thought about suffering and configuring it into a good. I came to terms with suffering too, not denying its reality, but seeing it as less of an impediment to pleasure and happiness—and certainly not as a builder of virtue and character. Christians were especially successful in seeing suffering as something to be transcended in the life, death, and resurrection of Jesus and also as a model for life ever after in a heaven that was a respite from human suffering.

"My teachings were a threat to both the Stoics and the Christians— at least in those times—and had to be exorcised. This was mainly successful until the rediscovery of Lucretius's poem in 1417. You Renaissance and Enlightenment fellows certainly were taken with the poem; I assume that is why you took inspiration in its resuscitation and re-crafted it to support Renaissance and Enlightenment themes placing humans at the center of the universe and savoring an attention to nature and knowledge. My teachings were almost lost again in the slogan "Eat, drink, and be merry, for tomorrow you may die." The worst part of it is that I never said anything like that—popular myths are certainly fascinating! I think it is time to correct the record and find a new vitality for my teachings, perhaps even reconciliation with Christianity. You attempted that and became a founder of what many believe to be an exceptional nation. Perhaps together we can revive my teachings in a way that speaks to that reconciliation."

Jefferson responds: "Your thoughts resonated deeply with me, although I ended up being very political—which you were not. I was always of two minds about embracing politics, but our American situation and the times were compelling. Even your piety impressed me—and, of course, your materialism. I became so fascinated with your materialism that I could not stand church doctrine and spirituality that denied the importance of the material world and distracted Christianity from the moral center of Jesus's teaching. That is why I produced the Jefferson Bible—to extract the moral teachings of Christ and separate those from the more fantastical elements of the Jesus story in the Christian Bible. Some think that I, like you, am an atheist—but that is not true. You gave proper attention to the gods in the temples as I did as a regular church-goer."

Epicurus interrupts: "My materialism stemmed from my practical realism, as did yours. There is really life after death in my teachings, just not individual immortality. Atoms are set free in the creative destruction of death and decomposition—free to be reorganized and find new shapes. Perhaps I could have been a Hindu and believed in reincarnation—these Asian religions do not seem as enamored with doctrinal subtleties or clerical control. But they do not pass my test of avoiding illusion. I would be unsatisfied with these religions except that the mindfulness preached by the Buddhists is certainly attractive on one level. However, I would like to focus on the good life and practical wisdoms, not paradoxes. Knowledge must be pursued with vigor, and illusions must be exploded—even when that is unsettling.

"You and I, Thomas, were crucial to the formation of the modern self—don't you think?"

Jefferson responds: "I think you are right, although this modern preoccupation with consciousness can get very complicated. The philosopher Charles Taylor has said that in the last several centuries 'a new kind of reflection' focused on self-explanation and self-knowledge has developed. This is the modern self to which we both contributed and with which I am comfortable—a practical realism that stimulates human achievement, is simple and direct, and looks to nature as our lodestar. Your practical wisdom of confronting illusions reemerged decisively with the discovery and circulation of Lucretius's poem after 1417; confronting illusion and fears is exactly what was needed to help break us from the grip of those who feared the rise of reason and science."

Jefferson hesitates a moment before continuing: "My own role in all this, besides relying on your teachings, was to pen the language of life, liberty, and the pursuit of happiness. Ironically, it was an adaptation of Locke's formula of life, liberty, and property. This entire happiness idea has just exploded—I know I could not have come up with it without you, but I still have to wonder about it and what it means. You are clear about happiness and pleasure, but I think there has to be a base of meaning that overlaps pleasure and happiness but is not coterminous with either of them. Meaning and happiness overlap but are not the same thing, as this younger generation of millenials seems to know well. I knew that when I distinguished life and liberty from happiness and qualified happiness with 'pursuit of,' since it is so hard to guarantee happiness. Strangely, Locke's formula was congenial to me because property and happiness seem to go together—although I made a mess of it with owning slaves. I could have used you more to overcome the self-delusions that came with that. It always tormented me and left some stains on my historical record."

Epicurus interjects: "Of course I, too, was so wary of struggles like you experienced. That is why I was so careful of the claims of sexuality and the gyrations of politics and ambition. You did not hesitate much on these fronts, Thomas, but I detect that you were aware of the complexities each brought forth."

Jefferson responds: "You are so right, and I want to explore all this more thoroughly with you as a test of character. Now that I have you here, I suggest we probe further by choosing a favorite quote of the other and asking the other to reflect on its meaning. This will help us find how this triad of life, liberty, and happiness can really work."

Epicurus responds: "An excellent idea. You first: Which of my quotes would you throw at me to get this started?"

Jefferson answers: "One of my favorites is 'Let no one be slow to seek wisdom when he is young nor weary of it when he has grown old. For no age is too early or too late for the health of the soul.'"

Epicurus reflects: "Seeking wisdom should be a constant of humans not limited to the old nor denied to the young. Perhaps when we are young, wisdom seems unattainable or confining. The energy of the young may make them seem disorderly, but I have always thought disorder is not a negative and can be concentrated on as it occurs, whether in the wonder of a thunderstorm or of raging seas or the hormones of youth. Sure, tranquility can be a goal, but even the young see the cycles of turbulence and relative peace that alternate in their own lives. And they are curious because of the freshness and excitements of life. Sensations are how we make contact with reality. The young know this very well.

"The old may think their time is past, but the greatest wisdoms are in confronting fear of death. The young think that they are invulnerable and hence do not fear death. Wisdom may come more easily when fear of death is not present, so the young may have an advantage on this front. The old may begin to fear death without realizing how much of life is really left. But there is wisdom in the old—fear of death may be there, but there is so much experience to draw on. God or the gods may be feared, and the infirmities of aging may be present; still, the joys of children and grandchildren can balance these agonies. But the real test for developing wisdom is how to slow the seeming velocity of life and nurture the right sensibilities in the last chunks of one's life. Piety may help, but a focus on amplifying the last bits of life in their pleasures, both high and low, is a great opportunity for wisdom seekers.

"Now it is my turn to cite a favorite quote of yours. At first it seems to counter mine. You said, Thomas, 'Truth advances, and error recedes step by step only.'"

Jefferson responds: "I see why you think it may be contrary to your quote. Mine seems to imply that we can accumulate knowledge only over a prolonged period of time and learn incrementally from experience. This may be true of the pursuit of knowledge. But wisdom, especially practical wisdoms, is of a whole different order. Information can overwhelm knowledge, and that is why truth has to advance slowly and methodically. But even though truth advances slowly, everyone—even the young—needs practical wisdoms to navigate life. The needs are now and not in some far-off time when knowledge and truth will somehow be more present.

"It is easy to say that there is a logical progression from information to knowledge to wisdom, but it need not be chronological. I kept meticulous records on crops, seasons, and weather at Monticello, but I still needed a way to organize and make sense of all of that information. More information did not always help explain what was going on; context had to be supplied. Knowledge is what they now call an 'aha' moment—getting all the pieces together and seeing them in a new way. Wisdom is about the right use of that knowledge and the courage to use it in the appropriate moments while appreciating the emotions and perceptions of others with similar knowledge. You, of course, know all this. I was so impressed with your sense that fear could keep us from acquiring knowledge and could impair our judgment and willingness to act. Wisdom is always practical, in your view and mine; the sources of wisdom can be many, but it all seems to come down to the courage to develop knowledge and use it rightly. Even the young know that, and the old may have to relearn it if they have lost it.

"Epicurus, your comments on getting the most out of life struck me strongly. I had a very full life even when relatively young, and even after my presidency I had much to do. I thoroughly enjoyed retirement. There was tranquility about that, but it was not about leisure or removal from the world. Retirement offers an opportunity to develop, as the archbishop of Canterbury said recently, a 'meditative attitude that…underlies wisdom.' There is vigor in this, and I believe your critics were wrong in seeing your notion of tranquility as too passive or unengaged. Wisdom requires courage to act, and certainly practical wisdoms are needed for a philosophy of living—perhaps even more needed in the last bits of life. Take, for example, my reconciliation with John Adams and the prodigious correspondence of the two of us after my presidency. Retirement combined energy and tranquility into creative, satisfying activity.

"Now it is my turn to see how you react to another of what I consider to be your most profound maxims: 'Of all the means which wisdom acquires to ensure happiness throughout the whole of life, by far the most important is friendship.'"

Epicurus responds: "This I said way before Facebook! If we only had patents back then! Seriously, friendship is not as easy as it first seems. We all have many acquaintances, but where is that point where acquaintance spills over to friendship? This is where wisdom tells you to have courage—courage to be open to another, to be vulnerable, and to be able to handle the knowledge that the other person can know you as well as, if not better than, you know yourself. And there is the reciprocity—not just in conventional things like gift giving, but in being able to share the joy of what you called an 'aha moment,' to see the world from similar vantage points even if you have different backgrounds, life histories, or even different values. But that shared 'aha moment' does not guarantee a sustained relationship. Joy has to be furthered by mutual commitments to each other, not just by sharing goals but by doing things together and reasoning together. Friendship is like family, although it takes more courage—courage to sustain a relationship that does not necessarily come from blood. Happiness is when you have the comfort of family and friends and the thought of being apart from either for too long seems more oppressive than separation itself. You know how I feel about fear—fearing separation is not healthy, but sensing tragedy in friendships or families need not disable us; it is recognition that life is precious and that happiness can be attained even under undesirable conditions.

"Which reminds me, Thomas, of another of your statements that I would love to hear you reflect on: 'Perfect happiness…was never intended by the Deity to be the lot of one of his creatures … but that he has very much put in our power the nearness of our approaches to it, is what I have steadfastly believed.'"

Jefferson responds: "History seems to suggest that life is one trail of tears after another, even if one does not fully embrace Hobbes's dictum of life as short, nasty, and brutish. But you were one of the first to turn this on its head by showing that pleasure, and avoiding pain, were possible and inherently desirable in tandem with each other. But you went even further and said that it should be central to a personal philosophy of living. And you made it practical and an honest reflection of sensory experience, not some Platonic form. Zen Buddhism apparently says something similar to you on pleasure and pain. There can be no perpetual bliss—negative moods need to be experienced and held in an emotional balance in order for us to be fully alive.

"Perhaps more important in that quote is my deference to a god with good intentions toward humans, even if that god does not expect perfect happiness for them. There is a historical movement in the great monotheistic religions to begin seeing god as benign, even as a god of love and compassion. This is remarkable and spills over to society. We are now validated in our optimism, and hope becomes something more real—not just a notion to soothe suffering. And I used the word *power* on purpose, too. God is sharing power, and we humans begin to figure out how to gather and use more of it. Whitehead even stated that humans have as much of an effect on god as god does on us. This thinking can challenge some traditional elites who like using god or gods to increase their own power, or at least protect the power and privileges they have. But when people can develop knowledge and wisdom on their own, they begin to realize the power they have. This can be very dangerous to outmoded elites.

"But back to my main point: Happiness is not only possible but *very* possible. Progress occurs—not in a straight line, and often by turbulence or at least with a swerve you ancient Greek atomists talked of. And we can use that turbulence to propel further progress. What is progress anyway but our ability to pursue happiness as far as any generation can imagine.

"And now it is my turn to pitch another of your quotes for your comment. You said that 'self-sufficiency is the greatest of all wealth.' I'd love to hear how you tease out that bit of practical wisdom."

Epicurus responds: "Learning how to deal confidently with one's basic needs empowers you and reduces tensions with those around you. You aspired to that here at Monticello by growing what you needed and manufacturing so much of what was required to run Monticello. You had wealth to purchase many pieces of art, fine furniture, and books, but you always knew that the self-sufficiency of farmers was of great value to society at large. And you always kept a focus on self-sufficiency—showing yourself to be a follower of mine.

"I was especially intrigued by your unsuccessful efforts to grow wine grapes and make wine, particularly since you knew so well the pleasures and advantages of wine. It must have been hugely frustrating for you, just as it must be highly satisfying to now see so many fine, well-run wineries so close to Monticello."

Jefferson interjects: "It is not only satisfying but a complete joy—so close to perfect happiness. I can wander on a horse and visit two dozen with relative ease. And the quality of the wines, so reminiscent of my beloved Burgundy and Bordeaux regions, is a real testimony to what human inventiveness and commitment to excellence can do. Marry that with the natural beauty of this region, and something profound is at work."

Epicurus continues: "What you said about coming close to perfect happiness, but not quite getting there, is true of self-sufficiency, too. We do not want to isolate ourselves in a Robinson Crusoe way. After all, friendship is also valued, and friends can help each other. I do not see these values in conflict with each other—self-sufficiency and friendship can complement each other. It reminds me of those who think my notion of pleasure as tranquility is not ambitious or energetic enough. But tranquility can have a very focused core dedicated to reasoned discourse, the demands of friendship, and the study of nature. The excitements and possibilities of nature alone can drive one to a joyous mental frenzy and an ambitious vision."

Jefferson interrupts: "Epicurus, what was your life's vision?"

Epicurus: "It certainly was not the industrial revolution or consumerism. I looked to the flow of nature for moral inspiration. My vision was much closer to the Romantic school of the nineteenth century. Wordsworth said, 'The landscape is the scene of human life.' There is a poetry of nature—Lucretius assuredly captured that. My vision was close to that of the scientific revolution as it connects to the current environmental movement. I saw science and morality as combined—that a moral impulse could be derived from a physical law. I saw movement in nature—I saw it driving intuition and understanding. Even though I know each person's life is only brief, its brevity does not mean living sedately. Self-sufficiency and tranquility were not meant to be decadence. They were meant to position us to examine nature and rely on each other. The movement and velocity of nature are exciting—we have to put ourselves in a position to hold that stream of activity so that we can understand it. A dam cannot hold the stream of nature forever; but we are like a dam that can hold long enough so as to feel the turbulence that eventually breaks through."

Epicurus pauses and then continues: "I am intrigued by the debates among the anthropologists about what distinguishes us from other animals. Ernest Becker argues that it is the awareness of death. How we deal with this awareness is crucial, then, and that is why conquering the fear of death was so central to my philosophy. It also explains why the evolution of the Christian formula for conquering death seemed so contrary to mine in early Christianity. Practical wisdoms can confront that Christian formula better than atheism, don't you agree, Thomas?"

Jefferson responds: "I agree, practical wisdoms privilege the flow of life. One of my practical wisdoms was religious tolerance, and I even permitted a Christian chapel just outside the main part of the University of Virginia. 'Live and let live' seemed far more practical than fighting among religions or developing a belief in atheism. You and I both believed in the wisdom of piety as a practical matter of participation in community and blessing the passages of life. Piety without deep belief in an afterlife does not seem to shake religious establishments. Ironically, it seems to shake this current crop of atheists more."

Epicurus continues: "But back to my life's vision. I saw self-sufficiency as the positive side of eliminating the fear of death. Good things are most possible when the focus is on life and a confidence that we do not need much, that reason is our tool, and that a modesty about human achievement are all valuable. I say this even as I marvel at your achievements—which brings us to the point where I want to hear you reflect, Thomas, on one of my favorites of your quotes: 'Nothing gives a person so much advantage over another as to remain always cool and unruffled under all circumstances.' It seems to be another way of establishing self-sufficiency."

Jefferson responds: "You did not choose to live in the fiercely competitive world I did—and I was often at the epicenter of it. But staying cool and unruffled has the same qualities as your self-sufficiency—being able to stay in control of oneself helps to control others. There were times during the American Revolution when the Brits almost caught me at Monticello, and the political debates of the 1790s were as awful and personalistic as one hears today in the nation's capital. And being cool and unruffled does not always work. President Obama certainly has that reputation for being cool, but it only occasionally is advantageous for him.

"Another way of looking at it is similar to your notion of tranquility; if you are cool and unruffled it might seem you are tranquil. But it can be just a mask for a seething energy below—much like, as you indicated, the restless waters beneath the surface of a lake behind a dam or the old saying 'Still waters run deep.'"

Epicurus interrupts: "Ah, but it is not superficial. Tranquility requires depth and has to have an authority and power at least equal to that of fear and pain."

Jefferson continues: "Fascinating. It is like what I see from the winery owners and winemakers of this region now, fiercely competitive but very civil and attuned to the voice of the land. If they stay cool and unruffled, it keeps the competition from being destructive. Even when anxiety over the grape harvest seems greatest, they convert it into a positive excitement. The small terroirs of the wineries seem to create a larger terroir of professionalism and pride in the region. I see something I really like here: an attention to detail and to perfectibility, much as I had in my days at Monticello. I would like to think that my legacy has had something to do with that. Whether this entire Monticello appellation can be said to have a terroir, I'll let the wine professionals debate. All I know is that this is one of the most exquisite examples of terroir outside of the hills of Burgundy (but I assume I will have to fend off contenders in Napa and the Willamette Valley!).

"Speaking of terroir, American wine critic Matt Kramer writes that 'hearing the voice of the land is sweet and you will not easily forget it.' This Monticello region cannot be forgotten. Even before the wineries it was special, and my university has become renowned. It is even a World Heritage site, and the graduates hold a special affection for the university, Charlottesville, and environs that is extraordinary. You must have anticipated that by planning your visit with me. I should have known when you quoted Wordsworth earlier: 'The landscape is the scene of human life." And what a landscape we have here! Look what human life has done, not only in preserving so much of it but in the inventiveness that is clearly evident in the university, the wineries, and the commerce of this region.

"So the point is, I guess, that if we all stay cool and unruffled there can be the best for all: rivalries held in check and progress pursued. If only the political world had that more often. But I really like the balance of power you just suggested between tranquility and happiness on one side and suffering and fear on the other. Keeping cool and unruffled

stabilizes and makes it possible for tranquility and happiness to dominate the balance. This is a practical wisdom of yours, Epicurus, which is
profound and overcomes your critics. You really were attentive to power
in the personal sense, and that is where social power must emanate.
Santayana thought you cared only for 'the muffled pleasures of the wise
man,' but you had to create a dynamic and robust counter to the fear
and pain that can decimate humans. You clearly value more than 'muffled pleasures'—there is a vitality that leaps out from your philosophy,
an energy that people are drawn to in almost every generation as they try
to figure out how to live long and well.

"Enough of my philosophizing! I need to hear from you, Epicurus,
on this topic because you said, 'The greatest obstacle to pleasure is not
pain; it is delusion.' I hope I am not delusional because of my attraction
to your notions of pleasure!"

Epicurus responds: "You are not delusional, although reconciling
the contradictions between your love of liberty and your ownership of
slaves must have been daunting to you personally. Much ink has also
been spilled on this, but I think I need to show you why this balance of
power you seem so enamored with is more complicated than you think."

Epicurus turns to Jefferson's ghost, looks him straight in the eye,
and says: "Happiness and pleasure have more than the two enemies of
fear and pain in my teaching; the more powerful enemy is delusion. And
it is even more complicated than delusion teaming up with fear and pain
as we often see in religious doctrine; it can also team up with tranquility
and happiness, not only in religious myths of heaven and paradise, but
also in myths that accumulation of things can guarantee happiness. You
understand this at some level, Thomas, or you would not be as dedicated
to my philosophy as you have professed."

Jefferson responds: "You are right, Epicurus. Finding a philosophy
of living that narrows the gap between our present and desired future
selves is difficult and often filled with rationalizations. Look at all the
New Year's resolutions that are broken so easily each January. There has
to be set of practical wisdoms that helps us."

Epicurus replies: "There is, of course. There is a power in a set of wisdoms that is beyond that of a given resolution one can make. And the most important point to make here is that delusion is far more destructive when it is in alliance with fear and pain than when it is allied with tranquility and happiness. It is much easier to unpack when delusion aligns with pleasure, but only if you have a philosophy of living that clearly counters excesses of pleasure. You appreciated that, Thomas, even though it can be difficult to implement. That is why a clear, convincing set of practical wisdoms is necessary—a set that is designed to capture who you are, that is explicit, and that you can share with others before you die. You articulated that well when you spoke of the need to explain oneself to others before one dies—even if you did not fully rise to that particular challenge."

Jefferson responds: "A missed opportunity, I'm afraid, but one that will lead to even more books about me than I could ever have imagined. Perhaps I am what the biographer Joseph Ellis has called me: the American Sphinx."

Epicurus continues: "I knew the power of delusions, particularly when they are in an unholy alliance with fear and pain. But it has become worse in recent times, I'm afraid. Humans have known about delusions and illusions for eons, whether rationalizations, lies, or magicians who fool us. But these moderns have raised it to new levels with their ideologies and especially their marketing prowess. Susan Jacoby recently wrote about this in her book *Never Say Die*, in which she describes in detail the illusion of happy old age sold by marketers. Now, at one level, happy old age may seem Epicurean, but I never suffered under the illusion that old age was a time of great happiness. We know that the infirmities of the very old can be debilitating, even as we have seemed to add a whole new third to our lives in the prosperous countries. We need a philosophy of living that not only attempts to defer our date with death but also—and primarily—makes best use of the time we have. These marketers are compounding the delusion of a happy afterlife with delusions of constantly happy 'golden years.' That is why

I insisted that when the fullness of happiness and pleasure cannot be found, tranquility is 'good enough.' But it is not a tranquility that makes a virtue out of suffering; it is a tranquility that confronts delusions energetically.

"It is my turn to choose one of your maxims for you to comment on. And it seems to follow naturally from a discussion of delusion. You said, Thomas, 'He who knows best knows how little he knows.'"

Jefferson responds: "At first it seems paradoxical, but it is not. There is so much to know, and the more one learns, the clearer it becomes that there is far more to learn. Your study of nature had that dynamic—you pressed and probed to unravel mysteries knowing full well that more and more mysteries would show themselves or invite our detection."

Epicurus interjects: "Precisely—processes of change are always present. A Yale psychologist, Frank Keil, speaks of the 'illusion of explanatory depth.' Yes, I know another illusion to be confronted! Keil says we feel we know how a complex system works, but our understanding is superficial."

Jefferson continues: "Others have said much the same thing. Whitehead asserted that 'knowledge shrinks as wisdom grows.' Much of what we think we know is overturned by new knowledge—that is what the scientific method is about, and that is what a wise person knows. And the wise person's knowledge of this is more certain and unchangeable than most knowledge.

"A college president said something similar thirty-five years ago. He quipped: 'Half of what we teach is wrong—the worst of it is that we have no idea which half it is.' This made me laugh when I first heard it, but it confirms what we have been saying. This wisdom should not be used to assume that we know nothing or that it is a waste of time to pursue knowledge. Modesty and reason should align as knowledge increases. And modesty should be applied to reason itself so that we do not get too far ahead of ourselves as knowledge increases.

"Before we end, I'd like to return to the topic of living long and well. My next quote of yours for you to expound upon is as follows: 'That death is nothing to us makes the mortality of life enjoyable, not by adding to life a limitless time, but by taking away the yearning after immortality.'"

Epicurus responds: "Yes, we have touched on this several times, but it is of importance to all those who are aging and deserves much more attention. And that includes this huge generation of baby boomers. I know you have been fascinated by generational change, so your interest is again understandable, my friend.

"I have said frequently that death is nothing to us because all our sensations cease at death. There is nothing therefore to fear in death because pain ceases. Mortality of life is an occasion to be celebrated, not abhorred; we are not gods even if we figure out a way to live longer. We should then see life as something to be enjoyed because fretting about it diminishes enjoyment. Author Anaïs Nin said it even more beautifully than I: 'People living deeply have no fear of death.' Nin got it right. If you live life with gusto, the fear of death naturally evaporates. Look at the growing popularity of Halloween—live well, celebrate, play like ghosts, laugh, be with friends, and the fear of death can be conquered. Of course, I have also warned about the dangers of having too much of a good thing. A wise person knows this, but a wise person also knows, as Julia Child said frequently, paraphrasing former United States ambassador to France Horace Porter: 'Everything in moderation, including moderation.' I wish I had said that, because too often close observers of my teachings have interpreted them as leading to a diminishing zest for life. But there is a powerful dynamic in the flow of life. Live prudently, but not too prudently. You certainly understood this, Thomas."

Jefferson interjects: "So many of us were attracted to your teachings because of the study of nature and Lucretius's beautiful poem about you, 'On the Nature of Things.' The zest of nature is evident. Your philosophy did also prescribe prudence because pleasure can threaten pleasure itself. There is so much that is zestful in your interests and your attention to friendship, in particular. But I would like you to explain further why you are so taken with Julia Child's quote."

Epicurus responds: "I believe Julia Child was a hedonist, as am I, but a very careful hedonist. There is nothing wrong with this as long as you pay attention to your long-term self-interest. Aristotle and I disagreed on this, of course. I identified happiness with pleasure—and he did not. Humans value pleasure for its own sake—every baby knows that. My followers know that tranquility was important to me, but pleasure is the bigger part of happiness. The balance and combination of tranquility and pleasure are a work of a lifetime. Tranquility and moderation can only trump excess pleasure—that is why Julia Child's quote struck me so. She found just the right balance."

Epicurus continues: "This leads me to inquire about one of your more tantalizing quotes. You described retirement as the 'ineffable luxury of being owner of my own time.' What exactly did you mean by that?"

Jefferson responds: "It is quite simple, really. Most people feel this way if they plan well. If they do not, they can become bored or fritter away their time—on gambling, for example. Before retirement, the claims of colleagues, work, family, and even friends can make it hard to pursue some pleasures. The demands of work and family often diminish friendship except for work friendships. There is nothing particularly wrong with those, but friendships and family need to be nourished in retirement. The best way to proceed is to be philosophically minded and have a conversation with oneself about pleasure and wisdom. So many religions encourage meditation, but it has to be grounded in desire. Eastern religions often seem to want to eliminate desire—but meditation can concentrate our attention on the right combination of desires and wisdom. You and I have always believed the pursuit of a set of practical wisdoms was the best conversation with oneself."

Jefferson continues: "Your simple yet direct attention to desires always intrigued me. You taught of three types: natural-necessary, natural-unnecessary, and vain desires. My desires to be owner of my own time and to have a conversation with myself—how do they fit your categories, if at all?"

Epicurus responds: "Those desires are a prerequisite to friendship—you have to know and love yourself before loving friends fully. These are not vain desires like fame. They are not natural-unnecessary desires like luxury food and drink. They are clearly natural-necessary desires and deserve precedence over all others. Owning your own time is really about sharing it well, and friendships are crucial. I know we agree deeply on that, although I am concerned by your reference to an 'ineffable luxury.' What did you mean by that? It seems to suggest that it is not a natural-necessary desire."

Jefferson responds: "It was only a rhetorical gesture to emphasize the great pleasure of slowing the velocity of life. And slowing the velocity of life was so important for me because I needed a conversation with myself to refine wisdom and know myself so that I could thrive with family and friends. I usually pursued this on horseback or on my long walks. I often spent my time, as I walked or rode, rehearsing what I might want to share with friends later over a meal and a glass of wine or in a letter. I needed to know better first what was in my own mind. It had some qualities of daydreaming, but we now know that daydreaming can be central to creativity. I often thought of my desires, how to balance them and pace the flow of satisfying them. I had to ask what I really wanted. In my case, I focused perhaps too much on natural-unnecessary desires. I had so many—good food, fine wines, constant remodeling of my home. None of them were really necessary, but I rationalized them in part by sharing with friends. It troubles me that I consider myself an Epicurean but was often preoccupied with natural-unnecessary desires. These conversations with myself were often tortured—perhaps I should have returned to Locke and pursued property rather than happiness. Should it have been different for me, my friend?"

Epicurus replies: "You need not feel guilty, Thomas, for pursuing pleasures and desires. That is why I wish I had said what Julia Child and Horace Porter asserted about moderation in all things, even moderation. There never should be guilt about the proper pursuit of pleasures and happiness, and practical wisdoms are designed by each person to accomplish this. Julia had hers, and each of us should have our own, too. You made the same point, really, in the Declaration of Independence about life, liberty, and the pursuit of happiness; it is about living long and well, empowered by practical wisdoms and free to pursue happiness. That is the formula that historically has resonated so well, not only in this country but also around the world. The only moral claim for a person following the formula is to avoid hurting others and to minimize one's own pain; the former is hard to know because of unintended consequences, the difficulty of communicating well, and the dangers of hubris. The moral claim is rather simply stated but hard to execute. That is why the notion of freedom is open to so much contestation—we do hurt others when we pursue independence as a person or as a nation. Thomas, you understood much of this when alive, and philosophers and social scientists to this day are preoccupied with these matters. I guess I am more interested in how you minimized your own pain, since scholars and pundits will debate forever how and whether you really hurt others, whether northern businessmen, your slaves, or your women."

Jefferson responds: "I guess that is why in retirement I felt so good about being owner of my own time. I could avoid, but not entirely, the pains of regret and guilt. I valued those conversations with myself so much, particularly about competing desires. A multitude of desires arose even in my time because of prosperity, technology, and the expansion of a material world of great fecundity. I saw these as contributing to both my short- and long-term interests, and all were easy to obtain. The world I inhabited made possible both natural-necessary and natural-unnecessary desires. I am sure that was different in your time."

Epicurus agrees: "Yes, we had some wealth, but one could often live simply and well. Pursuit of natural-unnecessary desires seemed frivolous back then because they were typically about vanity, not the pursuit of happiness. By making pursuit of happiness so central, you were a genuine follower of mine. We want those of means to pursue pleasures properly without undermining those pleasures or harming others. And even if we are frugal in order to pass on our wealth to the next generation, we cannot guarantee that they will pursue pleasures properly. You owned your own time and used it!"

Jefferson says: "This sets up well my next pitch to you of one of my favorite quotes of yours: 'The wise seek to enjoy the time which is most pleasant and not merely that which is longest.' Please elaborate further on this."

Epicurus responds: "We do not know all of what a longer life can bring, but we know the pleasures that are proximate. Often people postpone pleasures until retirement only to find some disaster of infirmity or early death. Postponing gratifications I can see, but miscalculating the opportunities for actualizing them is a major error that my teachings deplore. Most pleasures, if kept simple, can be easy to satisfy. Postponing natural-unnecessary desires makes some sense—even though, Thomas, you were often tempted to pursue them vigorously. You pressed the envelope, as they say, and made your descendants postpone gratifications because of the precarious state of your finances upon your death. But they did not need to postpone natural-necessary desires, and that was my main point in making distinctions among types of desires. Both the pacing and the pattern of desires are important. Each type of desire requires a different pacing: soonest for natural-necessary; whenever, but preferably later, for natural-unnecessary; and vain—never! And the pattern—how the desires fit together—should be guided by one's set of practical wisdoms.

"Last, but not least, Thomas, is my call for you to explain one of my very, very favorite quotes of yours: 'When you reach the end of your rope, tie a knot in it and hang on.'"

Jefferson replies: "Well, it certainly is not about unnecessarily prolonging life; it's simply holding on to it to savor every last bit. It's like a bottle of wine—hold on to it until the very last drop comes out. Life, you know, is like a bottle of wine—its freshness and bouquet when opened and when the first sips are taken are like the excitements of youth. And the steady enjoyment of a bottle of wine in conversations with friends is like the joy of middle age—work, friends, and family array themselves with predictability and promise. But the last drops of wine pose a greater challenge: What we do in our senior years is to ponder the meaning of it all and the cultivation of wisdom we have gained from experience and reflection—particularly the practical wisdoms to be marshaled for our remaining time; that is the knot to be tied. And, as every sailor knows well, good knots are extremely valuable and essential for survival."

—∿—

With this, the ghost of Thomas Jefferson returns to his grave, and Epicurus's ghost seeks solace among the atoms of the universe.

—∿—

Epicurus and Jefferson can be sources of practical wisdoms, as can so many others. Using Epicurus and Jefferson was simply a device to tease out not only their practical wisdoms, but also like-minded others—like Julia Child. While one can dip into huge pools of potential and proven practical wisdoms, it can be congenial to rely on what I call "midwives"—a smaller number of sources that seem to speak to you. While not strictly needed (after all, a baby can be born without a midwife), this kind of source can help concentrate attention and—to mix metaphors—be like a maypole where candidate practical wisdoms can dance around before being finally chosen. The opportunity now is to model a process by which the selection process can play itself out. The example chosen is the result of my own search.

Your search does not have to be tailored to my personal example, of course. The key is to begin a diary of practical wisdoms that both intrigue you and connect to the rhythm and possibilities of your own life. Perhaps the easiest way to begin is by noticing and noting the number of practical wisdoms that are displayed in everyday life, including newspapers and human interest stories in various media. Then look at your own personal history and the prescriptions and wisdoms passed onto you by family and friends. Add the best words of advice and elegant sayings of mentors whether in your professional life, civic participation, or religious activities.

Once you have begun a diary, the next stage will be to integrate your potential selections into the rituals of the twelve drops in conversations over a bottle of wine. Start with just one practical wisdom to test it with a friend or companions. Articulate why you chose it and how it shapes your life. Listen as your friend or companions probe your selection and see how you defend it. It does not have to reach the status of a "maypole" –that can come later as you sharpen your search and look at how your practical wisdoms flow and how they cluster. Add a personal practical wisdom to your conversation at each gathering and encourage others to participate with their own. You may never need a maypole, but I believe it will develop as you look more deeply into sources of wisdom that speak to you.

Chapter 4

Shaping a Personal Set of Practical Wisdoms: An Example

There are many possible sources of practical wisdoms, but to shape an individualized set of practical wisdoms takes some effort and testing of candidates. There are shallow pools of maxims and pithy quotes that can be gleaned from the web. These can be just fine if they help you understand yourself and explain yourself to others. Deeper pools of wisdom can emerge from religious or philosophical traditions. My choice of Epicurus and Jefferson as deeper sources seemed appropriate to my exploration of the 12 drop experience, my own biography, and my stage of life.

The metaphor of the 12 drop rule is of the last drops of a life well led. Epicurus and his followers were an easy choice for me because they confronted the issue of death and immortality directly. But the pursuit of a useful set of practical wisdoms need not be limited to the old, as Epicurus has said. Any stage of life can and should generate practical wisdoms that we consciously and explicitly declare. To leave them vague or cluttered reduces the amplifications of life and definitions of character that give meaning and direction to the journey of living. This can apply to youth and the discoveries of sexuality, the worlds of ambition and work, and especially child rearing. There is virtue in seeking practical wisdoms from both deep and shallow pools, and there is additional virtue in writing them down during reflection and after conversation. There is a clarity that comes from such list making, which begins to rekindle the lost arts of writing a diary. Sharing the process via social media can become viral.

A diary of your practical wisdoms becomes a history of your search. Where did you go to find them? Which ones survived to make it onto your list, and which ones did not? Why? Did testing practical wisdoms in conversations with friends provide new insights? How often did the set of practical wisdoms shift, and what drove that shift? How difficult was it to establish the all-important flow of your practical wisdoms?

We are encouraged to measure and record in the modern world—from the foods we eat to our blood pressure and cholesterol levels, from our energy and water use to our bowel habits. Why not record the practical wisdoms that intrigue, pull, and explain us? It is simpler than it sounds, but the results can be profound. As Peter Drucker has said: "I learn only through listening to myself."

This kind of selection process is driven by the conscious selection of practical wisdoms that resonate deeply with the experience of an individual. But there is another pattern that applies: the rhythm, balance, and flow of the practical wisdoms. Practical wisdoms emerge through reflection and must be orchestrated. Their sequence and juxtaposition tell us as much, if not more, than even your most favored wisdom.

I entertained literally dozens of practical wisdoms, but my ultimate choices especially speak to me, and the set as a whole individualizes me. Before listing the ones I chose, I will give examples of those *not* included because one learns as much from those as from the ones selected. Perhaps one learns even more—as Sherlock Holmes taught us in solving a crime because of the dog that did not bark. And Peter Drucker again: "The most important thing in communication is hearing what is not said."

Below, then, are seven practical wisdoms that I found somewhat attractive but eventually chose not to include. The first four were relatively easy to discard, but the last three posed almost existential conflicts in my mind.

—⁓—

It's too early to say.
—Zhou Enlai

The Chinese foreign minister under Mao said this, allegedly in response to a question about the significance of the French Revolution. For a lover of history like myself, there is a beauty in thinking about history without rushing to definitive judgments. But some judgments need to be made in the flow of life and politics. The humor in Zhou's phrase is evident, and there is wisdom here—but just not a practical wisdom to me.

—⚒—

Well, the truth is there are simple answers. They are just not easy ones.
—Ronald Reagan

Reagan's quote seems to err in the opposite direction from Zhou's, but it is balanced by its assertion that effective action to achieve a goal is not easy. The modesty and humor of the statement are certainly attractive, but I selected instead, as you will see in detail soon, the Voltaire quote "The best is the enemy of the good" because it had more direction to it in helping one make judgments, especially those hard choices between attempting to achieve a highly desirable goal and "settling" for something else.

—⚒—

Life is under no obligation to give us what we expect.
—Margaret Mitchell

This held a great deal of attraction to me since it affirms realism and inoculates against developing illusions. But it did not provide enough energy to make more out of life or to stimulate the definition of, and movement to, a better self. Thus it was rejected for my list of top twelve practical wisdoms.

—⚒—

Anything could be a structure for one's energy.
—Valerie Block, in the novel *Was It Something I Said?*

This quote, on the other hand, looks more optimistic. It even seems to legitimize the effort of writing this book—using something as mundane as the last drops of wine to leverage philosophical musings. However, it seemed to be too open-ended, and I am not sure how many "anythings" one could possibly choose in a lifetime or what criteria one might use to select them. And when does the pursuit of one thing diminish the quality of pursuing something else?

—⁂—

Sticks and stones may break my bones, but words will never hurt me.

I have always liked this saying because it combined my aversion to violence with my appreciation of the tactical power of the defense mechanism of denying the power of words. There is practical wisdom in this old saying, but its frequency of use betrays the truth that words can really hurt. Not only do they hurt even when not intended to do so, but also the incidence of hurt due to words is much, much higher than that of physical violence. It is a given that physical pain leaves marks, but there are also psychological wounds from hurtful words. The defense mechanism of denying hurt associated with words may work tactically in a verbal dispute with another, but there is little contribution to a philosophy of living and the pursuit of happiness. While the tactical advantages of the saying have attractions, it lacks strategic staying power.

—⁂—

Friendship trumps all.
—Thomas Jefferson

This one seems so consistent with both Epicurus and Jefferson that to not embrace it could appear scandalous, given the structure of this book. But friendship does not really trump all, although it is essential to both pleasure and happiness. As we will see soon, it cannot really trump honesty. As a practical wisdom, friendship cannot prevail all the time because it can erode professionalism and other values. And as a practical wisdom, the statement cannot pass a test of precision because it does not give enough specific guidance for various situations. Practical wisdoms thrive, in my view, when they combine a coherent comprehensiveness and an action-oriented prescription, if only implicit. And of course, we want our practical wisdoms to be elegant—beautifully crafted but profound—and parsimonious—that is, lean and efficient. But this practical wisdom is just too lean.

—m—

Honesty is the first chapter in the book of wisdom.
—Thomas Jefferson

Wow! This one should almost be sacred, given my awe at the commitment to academic honesty represented in the honor code at the University of Virginia, Mr. Jefferson's university. Add that to my research and publications on academic integrity over the past twenty years, and one might be dismayed—or at least especially curious—about why it did not make my top twelve. Then combine that with an Epicurean commitment to confronting illusions, and it almost seems preposterous it did not make it.

Honesty itself does work as a standard to evaluate the potential of "Honesty as the first chapter of the book of wisdom." People lie and dissemble, and Bruce Handy in the *New York Times* in 2014 remarked on "our genius for self-deception." Confronting illusion is important, but honesty is a broader and tougher standard than confronting illusion—a standard that cannot withstand the onslaught of cutting corners, hyperbole, and rationalizations that fills the lives of humans, as persuasively argued by Jeremy Campbell in *The Liar's Tale*. So complete honesty is aspirational—trumped by Voltaire's "The best is the enemy of the good." Honesty may be the best, but it can often be the enemy of the good—so imply Barry Schwartz and Kenneth Sharp in *Practical Wisdom* when they speak of practical wisdoms as "moral improvisations." To embrace improvisation does not necessarily turn us into little Machiavellis; honesty does simplify life by helping us to avoid the misplaced energies of "the webs we weave when we practice to deceive."

Now that I have been honest about honesty, on to my chosen practical wisdoms.

—∞—

The Author's Top Twelve Practical Wisdoms

1. "The best is the enemy of the good."
2. "Build on your strengths and make your weaknesses irrelevant."
3. "Mistakes are our best teachers, so don't waste them."
4. "Good things happen to those who hustle."
5. "Elites rule; elites screw up."
6. "Everything needs to change, so everything can stay the same."
7. "I have a need of your need of me."
8. "Attention is the rarest and purest form of generosity."
9. "Spend more time with people who are happy."
10. "Don't sweat the small stuff."
11. "Compound interest is the eighth wonder of the world."
12. "Everything in moderation, including moderation."

—∞—

The best is the enemy of the good.
—Voltaire

I have already mentioned my reliance on this particular practical wisdom. Voltaire's wisdom has been recognized ever since his work was first published. Variations of this practical wisdom have surfaced powerfully in the works of economists and political scientists over the past several decades. Nobel laureate and economist Herbert Simon, for example, is known for his principle of "satisficing"—that is, choosing the first good path to getting to your goal rather than spending a great deal of time looking for the ideal path. Political figures such as Senator Edward Kennedy learned this practical wisdom after stopping President Nixon's health care plan, fearing it did not go far enough. Kennedy admitted his mistake in his last book, published shortly before his death. Decades of attempted health care reform since the 1970s have been frustrating and expensive (17 percent of US GDP goes to health care, compared with 10 percent in other developed countries), causing debilitating political crises and loss of confidence in government.

The reach of this practical wisdom is vast, covering not only policy analysis and decision- making, but also debates about income inequality and gender differences. For example, Kathy Kay and Claire Shipman, writing in the *Atlantic* in 2014, conclude that, unlike men, women have a perfectionism that gets in the way of building confidence.

This practical wisdom is not universally touted, however. Many idealists feel that stepping back from what is thought best diminishes the push for achievement and reduces proper ambition. A slippery slope of diminished expectations can lead to mediocrity—as so many professors sense in relation to grade inflation. But practical wisdoms cannot be absolute, nor are they rules. They are attentive to the courage to act, not the abandonment of action. They are attuned to the desirable *and* the possible. It is always crucial to think carefully about what is desirable *before* running off to what is possible. The dance of the desirable and possible requires close calibration and exquisite focus; it cannot be rushed, but it needs completion—that is why so much organizational life is driven by deadlines.

Now to my second practical wisdom.

—ɯ—

Build on your strengths and make your weaknesses irrelevant.
—Peter Drucker

This wisdom began with a realization that humans often spend too many of their energies focused on what they are not yet achieving rather than exploiting their talents and skills. Organizational theory recognizes that organizations can compensate for some individual weaknesses by combining the strengths of its employees.

For a given individual, some weaknesses do deserve attention. If a golfer is putting poorly, practice and lessons could produce handsome results. Like all practical wisdoms, Drucker's is not absolute. But it has utilities even for our golfer. He could be just a mediocre putter but may have strong skills as a chipper. Building on that strength to get even closer to the pin decreases the length of putts, thus increasing the probability that our golfer will make them.

Using this practical wisdom can be as simple as applying the economic principle of comparative advantage. This principle states that even though one person may have an absolute advantage in doing/making everything, there still is an advantage in a division of labor when one specializes in an area of relative advantage or efficiency.

Or it can be as complex as understanding the emotional strengths and vulnerabilities in a personal relationship. One person can be compassionate and the other reserved. The more compassionate one can build on this empathy to better appreciate the more inscrutable other. The one who is reserved can build on listening strengths to appreciate the generosity of the other. Balancing the emotional strengths in a relationship can reinforce what is already promising. Weaknesses are not necessarily destructive in relationships, but knowledge of them is significant. They are relevant and can be transformed into strengths. Thus we learn yet again that practical wisdoms are not absolute, but thrive because of their improvisational qualities suited to practical situations.

—∞—

Mistakes are our best teachers, so don't waste them.
—Norman E. Rosenthal

The third practical wisdom I selected continues the flow of the first two. It is not good to be overly preoccupied with strengths; we must learn from what has gone wrong. Athletes refer to being "in the zone"—a place where strengths have been so internalized that incredible productivity is smoothly delivered and mistakes averted. It is more than learning from mistakes—it is making sure that mistakes actually teach us. It is what *New York Times* columnist Frank Bruni calls nurturing a "seasoned mind." He states, "Life is about learning to look past what's lost to what's found in the process." It's about, then, finding a pivot between a deep knowledge of excellence and what we have painfully learned from our mistakes. The pivot has an excitement to it that cannot be easily sustained; we say we are in a zone because it is impossible to stay there forever. So enjoy it while you can, and look forward to positioning yourself for it the next time it comes. Csikszentmihalyi refers to this positioning as a "freely chosen discipline." It is not driven by a fear of mistakes but by a deeper knowledge that more is possible. It is a flow experience driven by practice and possibilities—knowledge that a plateau of performance can be transcended, the mistake being to not want or not visualize it. To constantly transcend would turn us into gods, and it would be a mistake of hubris to aspire to that. And to learn humility—and combine it with a passion for achievement—means learning from the mistake of hubris but also from the mistake of low expectations.

While it is impossible to be always "in the zone," it is a mistake to think it can be simply chosen. It is likewise a mistake to think we can learn more from success than from failure. Success may set up a virtuous circle that feeds upon itself. There is not much to learn from this except about momentum and the fact that "trend is our friend." But a vicious circle has a similar momentum, except that the desire to break the momentum is far greater than in a virtuous circle. There arises a laser-like focus on what can break a vicious circle. The breaking of habits is admittedly difficult. But letting mistakes teach us is at the heart of breaking bad habits, even when we are repeating them. There is what I call an "effectiveness deficit" in breaking bad habits, a gap between what we know to be our mistakes and our ability to avoid them. What we must remember about the deficit is that others have had it, and we can learn from them in support groups or biographies.

So, is the glass half full or half empty? It is both and also could be something else. Willa Cather wrote in a letter: "Great people…somehow strike out the foolish platitudes that we have been taught to respect devoutly, and give us courage to be honest and free. Free to rely on what we really feel and really love—and that only." Practical wisdoms are not foolish platitudes if they authentically speak to us and describe who we are. The glass may have far more foolish platitudes than what columnist E. J. Dionne Jr. depicts as "platitudes with a purpose." Our mistakes would be in not pouring out the foolish ones and not being attentive to the platitudes with a purpose that are left. Our twelve drops remind us that even a mostly empty vessel can still hold much wisdom.

—∞—

Good things happen to those who hustle.
—Anaïs Nin

At an administrative retreat twenty years ago at my university, a speaker—who happened to be a medical doctor—told us that we should be making more mistakes in our careers at that time than we had a few years prior. He explained that the velocities of professional life were increasing, thus multiplying the opportunity for error, but assured us that this effect was usually benign. The psychological point he was making was that those of us who were perfectionists should just get over it. President Truman said much the same thing when he said we are all bound to make mistakes; we just have to make sure we can correct them later. Some mistakes are irreversible, but fearing mistakes reduces what can be achieved. Thus, there is a virtue in "hustling"—persistently and energetically going for your goals—rather than holding back.

This practical wisdom flows naturally from the previous one. But rather than examining the instructive power of mistakes, it contextualizes by explaining—and justifying—what drives us to make them. The virtues of achievement outweigh the costs of error. Hustling, then, is placing a goal—even that of personal gain—as an intrinsic driver of a work ethic.

Foreigners who visit America soon detect the energy of American society in both entrepreneurship and civic activism. This practical wisdom speaks to me not simply as an American but also because of my upbringing and temperament. Growing up on an Illinois farm, I developed a work ethic in which I pursued tasks quickly, both to impress my father and to just "get it done." That work ethic continued in my professional life, both in academics and in public service in Washington, D.C.

Hustling is more than networking or pretending to work. It is task driven, and task completion brings simple satisfactions or career betterment. It is about getting a personal reward for what you do without worrying about getting credit for your efforts. There is a "shrewd humility" in this. Good things happen when you hustle, even when someone else seems to get credit for it.

But what about retirement and slowing the velocity of life? Does that diminish the value of hustling? The answer is probably yes—so why would do I include this wisdom? Because it fulfills the Jeffersonian maxim of explaining yourself to others before you die, and one needs to hustle to clarify and establish that set of wisdoms that explain you. There really is no need for deathbed confessions or revelations. So "get it done."

—〰—

Elites rule; elites screw up.

Vilfredo Pareto, the Italian sociologist, wrote more than a century ago about the necessity and persistence of elites in ages of democracy and egalitarianism. Other Italian political thinkers, such as Guido Dorso, described what a healthy political class should look like and why circulation of elites should occur to maintain the vitality of a political class. The fact that elites rule is commonly known today, even if one does not embrace C. Wright Mills's notions of a cohesive, conspiratorial elite or a Marxian approach to a ruling class. So why is this particular practical wisdom so important to me? The answer is in the second half of the wisdom, which reminds us that elites do not deserve complete deference because they often make huge errors and do not seem to learn from them. I could not call myself a political scientist if I did not hold in front of me this particular practical wisdom.

But given the previous practical wisdoms, is there something special about elites not learning from their mistakes, in contrast to other individuals? In the first chapter, I described the balance of effectiveness and responsiveness, which is a consequence of a consummate set of practical wisdoms. Elites often cannot find the balance between the two, with either too much effectiveness or too much responsiveness. In the former case, goals are set that are too ambitious or conflict with other goals in a dysfunctional way. In the latter case, overresponsiveness swamps the ability to make difficult decisions that are needed to move in a desirable direction; populist politics ensue, and the passions diminish prospects for a reasoned approach to shaping the good life.

Demystifying elites is more problematic than it seems, even in an era of diminishing confidence in and respect for institutions, whether political, religious, or financial. The late Samuel Huntington of Harvard helped explain this in his classic book, *Political Order in Changing Societies.*

He argued that political and social changes occur at different paces in our current world, with social changes occurring more quickly than political change. The lag can cause crises that become hard for elites to manage. At first, elites command respect for the disproportionate shares of political, economic, and symbolic assets at their disposal. But in the absence of strong institutions that are adaptable, such as bureaucracies, courts, and parliaments, elites can find the lag between political and social change overwhelming. Individuals who are not members of elites also can find keeping up hard (just ask any senior citizen who has to rely on a grandchild for help on a computer). But when elites cannot adapt quickly enough, their stewardship becomes deeply threatened. And if there is no mechanism for recruitment of different and more adaptable elites, the entire society is susceptible to revolutionary change.

The practical wisdom of attending to the skills and foibles of elites is just a window, then, into the world of politics. In practice, we watch and listen to elites, but the broader world of meaning in which elites act cannot be appreciated simply by taking notice of—or pleasure in—their mistakes, failures, and foibles. Unless we develop a broader appreciation of that world of meaning, there cannot be a greater wisdom; wisdoms that are just tactical, although of some value, do not capture the strategic context of modern politics. We need something I call "aspirational realism," rooted in an appreciation of the forces and ideas that are current but without getting pulled into a world of mean ideologies or populist rage. Thus we transition to the practical, but more nuanced, wisdom of the dance of order versus change.

—◈—

Everything needs to change, so everything can stay the same.
—Giuseppe Tomasi di Lampedusa

The above quote from the novel *The Leopard* shows a nuance to the problem of change that is not captured in the previous practical wisdom. The irony is poignant here, and the quest for a deeper balance of effectiveness and responsiveness more profound. The author of *The Leopard* has discovered the awful sense of disorder that somehow must be managed. Charles Taylor said: "The Epicurean is the lack of order, or one resulting purely from chance." Jefferson, on the other hand, was a political animal. He saw that disorder offered opportunities for shaping a new order and find meaning and virtue in it.

Huntington would say that strong political institutions are the only way to produce order. But exactly how can one help create pockets of order when social change is more rapid than political development? Huntington said that strong institutions had to meet four criteria: adaptability, complexity, autonomy, and coherence. Adaptability is easy to see, but what about the other three? Humans frequently try simplicity, and meditation and mindfulness often lead to seeing simplicity as a virtue. But Huntington does not accept that because simple institutions, such as traditional monarchies, can be more easily overwhelmed than complex ones by rapid social change.

By autonomy, Huntington meant the ability of a political system to avoid being controlled by a social force like the economy or a religion. Most Americans do not believe in the autonomy of politics, thinking it is controlled by Big Oil or Wall Street, for example. The Berkeley political scientist Kenneth Waltz would have called this "reductionist" thinking—that is, explaining political behavior as a feature of something besides politics itself. The political scientist Hugh Heclo has argued persuasively that institutions are valuable when disorder seems dangerously prevalent. I find it compelling that institutions are virtually the only way by which "everything can stay the same." This does not necessarily privilege conservatism because "reform, reform, reform" are the bywords of successful institutions, just as "location, location, location" are the bywords of real estate.

Even though institutions are valuable, there is often a justifiable ambivalence about them. The philosopher Martin Buber saw this when he said that institutions are "outside"—that is, arenas where humans work and pursue various other aims in society. He contrasted that with a world "within," where human life is more deeply engaged and where one "recovers from institutions." Practical wisdoms cannot simply be about work and civic activity—there has to be attention to love and play. And this is where we get the sense of coherence that prevents disunity in our life, thus satisfying Huntington's attention to the fourth criterion for successful institutionalization. Thus we pivot to one of my longtime favorite practical wisdoms, the one that unifies and centers my life while inducing coherence.

—◊◊◊—

I have a need of your need of me.

I adopted this practical wisdom as an undergraduate student in Iowa while I was dating my wife-to-be. It became so central to us that my wife, Mary Ann, had it inscribed on the inside of my wedding band. The origins of this particular wisdom are lost to us now but probably lie in the existentialist movement that was so vibrant in the mid-twentieth century. Thinkers such as Martin Buber explored the connectedness of individuals in their intimacies and friendships. The limits of reason and rationality often underlined existentialism. A reframing of the ancient Greek devotion to friendship, somewhat separated from a devotion to reason, has a compelling quality to it—one that finds meaning in what is felt and in what I call a "dramatic empathy."

So much could be lost if these dramatic empathies could not be nurtured. But could we also lose connections to a wider world and to others beyond our reach? The social theorist W. Warren Wagar would argue otherwise. In_The City of Man he describes two cultural perspectives that dominate the philosophical thinking of the past two centuries: utopia and cosmopolis. By utopia he is referring to a small, almost perfect community of great emotional strength. By cosmopolis he was describing a place whose inhabitants have a deep thirst to participate in a culturally diverse, tolerant, and interdependent world. The two perspectives are not necessarily mutually exclusive and can complement each other. So my cosmopolitan habits and interests could—and do—find great meaning and satisfaction in this particular wisdom.

But there is meaning and satisfaction in the dramatic empathy of romantic love. Charles Taylor said, "My identity is defined by the… horizon within which I am capable of taking a stand." Despite the disappointments and risks of romantic love, the philosopher Simon May sees that the modern project is so infused with the compelling character of romantic love that our identities are embedded in it, taking on what traditional religion had promised: "to find salvation from everyday suffering and banality through a great ideal." He goes on to say that romantic love permits us to be "radically autonomous" and is therefore "central to forging, charging, and crucially endorsing our evolving identity."

But the practical wisdom of having a need of your need of me is not unconditional. May speaks of the vulnerability of this conditionality since it exposes us almost totally to the needs of the other.

Contrast this with the Golden Rule. It requires looking primarily into yourself and your needs. There is no dramatic empathy in that, only an acknowledgment that the other may have needs similar to yours. There is a narcissism here that can be considered healthy if it nurtures constant, realistic, and mature goals and interests. But much narcissism is not healthy; and even with healthy narcissism there is little passion in doing unto others as you wish them to do unto you. There is reciprocity and prudence but not passion. The Golden Rule may be good as a practical wisdom, but not good enough when you have the robust connectedness of having a need for your need of me.

Although Epicurus did not embrace the passion of romantic love as much as Jefferson did, both would have understood the deep strands of friendship. Love and friendship can combine more powerfully than the old song about love, marriage, horses, and carriages. Modern romantic love could use more conversation about love and friendship and somewhat less about love and sex.

And now to my eighth practical wisdom.

—◊◊◊—

> Attention is the rarest and purest form of generosity.
> —Simone Weil

This practical wisdom speaks to me profoundly, both as a continuation of the flow of the previous two and also as a great personal challenge—whether in marriage, work, friendship, or parenting. One of the claims of meditation and mindfulness is their ability to quiet and focus the mind. One of the claims of the 12 drop experience is that it induces us to take a deeper look into ourselves and to listen to others speak to the practical wisdoms so important to them.

Sociologists Jeffrey Dew and W. Bradford Wilcox have shown that couples who are especially attentive to each other are almost four times as happy in their relationship as others. Psychologist Eli J. Finkel says, "Those individuals who can invest enough time and energy in their partnerships are seeing unprecedented benefits."

We all know many of the reasons for being inattentive, whether the state of the economy, competing claims on our attention, or just a failure to execute our priorities well. The last of these is harder to accept than the others because it usually implies that we gave something or someone else a higher priority. This could be professional achievement, hobbies, or keeping up on Facebook.

But exactly why should we link attention to the virtue of generosity? I assume it has to do with a radical expansion of our notions of gift giving. When we give our fullest attention to a baby, we delight the child with our eyes, our smiles, our voices. Yet we lose much of that attentiveness after the baby grows up. We often find that same fullness of attention in romantic love (perhaps that is why many refer to their lovers as "baby").

Fullness of attention is hard to sustain, however, and giving presents often becomes a substitute for genuine attention, a notion captured by the old saying when receiving such gifts: "It's the thought that counts." This, in one gesture, diminishes the gift and reminds both the giver and the receiver of the greater power of attention in its "purest form."

—⟋⟍—

Spend more time with people who are happy.
—Andrew Weil

This practical wisdom flows quite naturally from the previous one. We know that greater attention to the other in a relationship dramatically increases the possibilities of happiness. The pursuit of happiness was central to Jefferson's thinking, yet pursuing happiness by spending more time with happy people can be difficult given the demands of children, the tasks of helping aging parents, or the need to contend with the frustrations of the workplace. There seem to be so many unhappy people we encounter in a day that finding those happy people may be like looking for a needle in a haystack.

These difficulties may help explain the attractiveness of Facebook friends, but that is not really about spending time with them. There are several ways to identify happy people, the easiest of which is to find couples who are especially attentive to each other and befriend them. Parents raising school-age children often find compatriots among the parents of their children's friends, for example. Seniors find time to kindle new relationships as they maneuver themselves through the myriad social opportunities of retirement. Participating in civic life or hobbies throws together people with a defining passion for social or personal improvement. And many Americans find connections in religious contexts.

Although there can be multiple opportunities to spend more time with people who are happy, this practical wisdom is not about neglecting those who cannot find happiness. It is about an aspiration. Aspirations are important and should not be dampened. Jefferson understood the power of aspirations, and it would be imprudent for us not to share his understanding. Positive psychologists tell us that a majority of people report that they are happy, so the aspiration may be more easily realized than one might think at first.

—◌—

> Don't sweat the small stuff.
> -Richard Carlson

This practical wisdom is particularly powerful. It is not about aspiration; rather it is about maintaining focus on what is important in the clutter of minor matters that fill the space around us. Often these appear compelling because they either yell out urgency or offer a slight to our authority or status. It is hard to keep focused on what is most important in such situations. Yet we need to retain focus on the goal and the mission or they will be obfuscated. This practical wisdom recommends maintaining discipline and maturity when there are no obvious advantages to doing so in the immediacy of the situation.

This wisdom comes, as does most, from experience. That is why I often used it when mentoring young people; my most frequent phrase with students or employees was "water off a duck" to capture the fervent value of not getting caught up in every little issue that beckons your attention. My academic discipline of international relations also speaks to "strategic dominance," the requirement to maintain your strategy despite what others are doing. This means avoiding being reactive. You need not fight every battle nor turn skirmishes into battles. Well-crafted strategic goals are required, and aligning the means to achieve those goals is essential. This practical wisdom values discipline, especially.

This practical wisdom also counsels patience—a trait not common in America. But does it legitimate toleration of acts of discrimination against minorities or women? Do some slights demand immediate attention? Yes, there are acts that need to be confronted, but judgment is required about exactly when, where, and how to do that with the greatest effectiveness. Civil rights activists, feminists, and human resource specialists—among others—spend much time and energy on this problem. Finding the balance between deference and assertiveness can be excruciatingly difficult, particularly in cultures where whistleblowing is hard to do yet rebelliousness is glorified. The contradiction here is both astounding and understandable. But that is why this particular practical wisdom can be so important. It provides a perspective and disposition to manage the contradiction. A combination of disciplined persistence and patience can be incredibly advantageous, particularly in cultures that undervalue them. This effectively sets up the flow into our eleventh practical wisdom.

—⟋⟍—

> Compound interest is the eighth wonder of the world.
> —Albert Einstein

Discipline and patience work in a variety of contexts. Einstein, a brilliant physicist and mathematician, understood this, and yet it at first surprised him when it came to personal finance. I did not find the Einstein quote until a decade ago. But a corollary, the rule of seventy-two, came much earlier to me. For those not aware of that rule, it simply means that taking seventy-two and dividing it by the interest rate will tell you how long it will take to double an investment with reinvested interest or dividends. For instance, at a rate of 6 percent, an investment will double in twelve years. There are some advantages to being in debt, of course, whether in acquiring a growing asset like a home or anticipating that inflation will reduce the burden of debt. But there also can be acceleration of wealth by compounding. And it can be particularly attractive when a 401(k) replaces the practice of pensions; money set aside early in a career can multiply significantly by retirement.

It is not that hard to follow this practical wisdom when one is raised to be frugal and also has the skills or education that can bring a reliable income. But what can one do if these conditions do not apply? Advocates of financial literacy bravely suggest that saving and compounding can still occur without these advantages. It is hard to share this optimism, however, in an age when student debt loads are growing and the promise of home ownership appears ephemeral to many. The practical wisdom still holds, though, even when a strategy to implement it is complicated.

The problem of student debt load is beginning to be over-whelming, however, with total student debt now greater than all cred-it card debt in America. Young people who cannot save lose sight of the eighth wonder of the world. As a retired professor, I find this especially disconcerting, given my affection for students and interest in their futures. And the consequences for the general economy are drastic, given that student loans are handed out without underwrit-ing criteria. The dangers of default on student loans grow, and the inapplicability of bankruptcy protection for most of these loans cre-ates a virtual servitude for those who are not thriving financially.

This problem is further exacerbated by growing economic in-equalities, especially in America. We used to think that economic growth would reduce inequality. But a well-researched new book by Thomas Pik-etty of the Paris School of Economics shows that history does not confirm that belief. He studied centuries of data and found that wealth increases far more than wages over extended periods of time, thus furthering in-equality. Compounding may be the eighth wonder of the world, but we may get too much of it.

So, given this pessimism, why did I include this practical wisdom? I did so because it explains me personally, not because it is easily ad-opted by all. I followed this practical wisdom because I knew of it and could. My retirement and finances are secure, and it would have been hard to accomplish that without the wisdom of compound interest. My presentation of a set of practical wisdoms in this volume was designed not as advocacy, but as a model of how to develop such a set. Every set of practical wisdoms is unique and reflects the temperament, disposition, history, and aspirations of a given individual. Practical wisdoms should be selected because of these factors, not necessarily as prescriptions for others.

—⚬—

> Everything in moderation, including moderation.
> —Julia Child (paraphrasing Horace Porter)

This practical wisdom came to me at the suggestion of my wife as I was writing this book. Unlike the previous practical wisdom, this one is so very new and fresh to me as an expression. Prudence and moderation have always been central to my philosophy of life, if not my philosophy of living. My wife knew of my disposition in this regard, and therefore there was no need to explain myself to her. You need not look far for sources of practical wisdoms; sometimes they just fall in your lap!

Although Epicurus likely would not have embraced this practical wisdom (despite my depiction otherwise in chapter 3), Jefferson would find it congenial. He was moderate about many things, although he was passionate about family, love, friendship, books, and wine—of course. Epicurus was passionate about friendship but apparently little else. Both Epicurus and Jefferson valued reason deeply, and with that came moderation—except that the expansiveness of Jefferson's interests tempered his moderation.

This practical wisdom has a versatility that Jefferson would have welcomed. It puts a premium on judgment regarding when and where to set aside the compelling quality of moderation. There is little that is proscribed in this practical wisdom. It opens your universe to possibilities while still privileging moderation. At first it seems paradoxical, but its comprehensiveness is what appeals to me. And it especially appeals to me because of its symmetry with my first practical wisdom, Voltaire's

"The best is the enemy of the good." Moderation may be the best prescription for living, but the good life needs some excitement, even a feast occasionally.

But Julia Child's practical wisdom does raise the important matter of consistency. How important is it? And is there hypocrisy in the apparent contradictions? Practical wisdoms often have convolutions. We have seen them throughout this book, even in the Golden Rule. Where some see logical or epistemological problems, others see a dialectic requiring conversation and an attempt to work one's way through an apparent muddle. Here it is useful to remember Epicurus's statement about wisdom being more important than philosophy.

Practical wisdoms, because of their brevity and accessibility, do seem to short-circuit philosophical processes. One of the key advantages of the 12 drop rule and 12 drop experience is the stimulus to exploration and conversation about given practical wisdoms. This new cottabus can be much like the original one, then—a platform for philosophically minded play and a way of developing sensibility somewhat short of the rigors of professional philosophy. The satirist Fran Lebowitz has said, "Great people talk about ideas…and small people talk about wine." The idea of a practical wisdom shared with others is the driver of this book, and our wine talk has been exceedingly modest; by Lebowitz's standard, we are coming to the end of the book in pretty good shape. Let's see how far we can go in chapter 5 to wrap up our journey through the idea of a new cottabus.

CHAPTER 5

THE NEW COTTABUS: REMEMBERING YOUR "PERSONAL TERROIR"

History makes wine; wine makes history.
—Michael Bowles

The journey of this book has taken us from the 12 drop rule through the 12 drop experience to specific searches for practical wisdoms. In Martin Buber's terms, we have moved from the physical "world of consistency"—the 12 drop rule—to a "world of sensibility"—the 12 drop experience. It is now time to take stock of this journey, digest it, and see where it might yet take us. So far, its key elements are as follows:

1. Curiosity about nature;
2. structuring a playful pause at finishing a bottle of wine (the new cottabus);
3. collecting practical wisdoms and shaping them into an individualized set;
4. slowly displaying your practical wisdoms in the companionship of others;
5. practicing your practical wisdoms and remembering them.

The book has provided examples for all of the above except for the last. Remembering is not easy, just as eyewitnesses are often unreliable. Dorothy Parker, poet and satirist, addressed the problem of memory in a way that is especially applicable to the new cottabus: "I might repeat to myself, slowly and soothingly, a list of quotations beautiful from minds profound; if I can remember any of the damn things." Writing them down helps, of course, but remembering deeply so that your practical wisdoms will constantly fortify you is something more.

There are many techniques to stimulate memory, and one may choose any that promise to be effective. This chapter suggests two in particular that enrich the quest for practical wisdoms and deepen them. This takes the flow of the 12 drop rule and 12 drop experience to a sense of place that anchors us and helps us visualize.

—⚬⚬—

Your chosen set of practical wisdoms is what I have called a "personal terroir"—metaphorically, your microclimate, landscape, and skills at shaping a philosophy of living in the pursuit of happiness. This should be as important to you as terroir is to a winemaker. You are like a winemaker, then, in listening to the voice of your personal terroir, respecting it and developing it to your taste. Others before have used the concept of a personal terroir, notably novelist Lauren McLaughlin in speaking of her New England roots. But my use of the term speaks primarily to an interior landscape that then seeks out a sacred geography exterior to the self. I have sharpened the notion of a personal terroir and reconnected it to wine in the 12 drop rule and 12 drop experience.

We need broader horizons, then, that give a context and meaning beyond oneself. Martin Buber would give that the name of "It"—a world separate from our body but nourishing it. Buber refers to this as a "graph of place" where one "perceives an ordered and detached world." He goes on to call this a "reliable world" whose "organization can be surveyed and brought out again and again; gone over with closed eyes, and verified with open eyes."

Ernest Hemingway knew of this when he said that everyone needs a special place—*querencia* in Spanish, *sanctuary* in English.

Our deepest memories are nourished in such places, and they are refined and held more dearly there. These places are like a sacred geography that is often a result of a pilgrimage—common in most cultures and celebrated from Chaucer to Martin Sheen in *The Way* to today's Muslim hajj.

The story of wine is immersed in place—in terroirs, appellations, and wine regions. According to Matt Kramer, there is a "mentality of terroir" that has its fullest expression in Burgundy. Kramer goes on to say that terroir is not just about the soil and microclimate of a plot of land; it is about all that is distinctive about the grapes grown there and the human element—the winemaker and the "soul" of a wine.

Thomas Jefferson certainly heard the voice of terroir when, as US ambassador to France in the late 1780s, he explored Burgundy. His favorite vineyards were close to Pommard, a village near Beaune in southern Burgundy. Jefferson's education in wine was led there by Étienne Parent, who became one of Jefferson's key wine merchants not only when he was in Paris but also when he returned to America. It is clear in Jefferson's writings that Burgundy was his sacred geography, alongside the sacred geography of his beloved Monticello.

Étienne Parent's winery still exists in Pommard and is now run by a descendant, Anne Parent. I spoke with Anne in May of 2012 and sipped wine with her in the same wine cellar that Jefferson would have enjoyed. Anne's passion about the terroir of her vineyard gushed forth like champagne when first opened. Her passion is grounded in "respecting the grape" and in the balance of all the elements of the terroir of her vineyard—microclimate, location, slope, and winemaker. The winemaker is crucial to the distinctiveness of a terroir, according to Anne. She compared it to the work of two chefs who have the exact same ingredients but produce different outcomes. The 12 drop experience is much like that—the physical consistency of the twelve drops and the different sensibilities displayed in the individual sets of practical wisdoms.

My travel to Burgundy in 2012 was a key catalyst to the writing of this book. It was then that I realized that a pilgrimage was learning the story of one's own life and that a sacred geography was just beyond, yet within my reach. This led my wife and me back to Charlottesville, Virginia later that year to reminisce and to explore more deeply the delightful facets of the now booming Monticello appellation.

Samuel Johnson stated that the function of traveling is "to regulate imagination by reality." The function of a sacred geography, then, is to refine imagination by the sensing of place. Travelers see, touch, smell, taste, and listen. We anticipate our pilgrimage and then experience it. We take photos to remember, and we fondly recall the favorite meals of the place. We also remember wine tasting in wine regions and recall the flavors and experiences when we return with wine or join wine clubs. Sacred geographies are steeped in memories. Attaching your set of practical wisdoms to a sacred geography makes it easier to bond them in your mind and reminds you that there are realities—especially pleasurable realities—that are beyond you but within your reach.

But before one can fully embrace a sacred geography, there should be an understanding of your personal terroir. The ingredients are your practical wisdoms, and you are the chef. Once you have prepared your recipe—your personal terroir—it should not be hard to remember the ingredients. It helps that the practical wisdoms flow well and that you meditate on one with each bottle of wine. "Practice, practice, practice" is as essential here as "location, location, location" is to real estate.

There are, then, two special ways of deepening your memory of your set of practical wisdoms that are suggested in this chapter: 1) attending to the flow and logic of your personal terroir, and 2) associating your personal terroir—your set of practical wisdoms—with the powerful images of a sacred geography.

—⚬—

Regarding the first of these, there is logic in the flow of my own practical wisdoms, for example. The first, "The best is the enemy of the good," establishes the strategy of my search—not expecting perfection but utility and meaning in each practical wisdom. The second augments the first by acknowledging weaknesses and yet being attentive to one's strengths. The third, that "mistakes are the best teachers," completes the first triad of drops by showing we can learn profoundly from our errors.

The next three hold together too, by speaking of hustling, elites, and building institutions. All these are about ambition, power, and purpose. The three following are about a personal life of needs, attention, and happiness. The last three are just valued maxims that stand out to me as especially compelling: tactics of staying cool, developing wealth, and enjoying life with the gusto of a Julia Child.

The secret of developing your set of practical wisdoms is in the flow and connectedness of the story of who you are and who you want to be. Remembering the story is much easier once this structure is in place, but it is OK to use other devices to remember it also—like the old reliable of writing it down.

—◊◊◊—

The second way of remembering has to do with associating your personal terroir with a sacred geography, but not just any sacred geography. The new cottabus, I assert, requires a wine connection. By a sacred geography I mean a wine region or appellation that has a special meaning for you personally. As you now know, for me it is the Monticello appellation of Virginia. The appellation is fairly new, dating primarily from the 1980s. There already was a Monticello vineyard in the Napa Valley that could have challenged the use of the Monticello name for a Virginia appellation. But Jay Corey, founder of the Monticello winery near the town of Napa, told me he decided not to challenge the use of the name in Virginia. Jay was raised in Virginia, had a deep reverence for Jefferson, and wanted the wine industry to prosper in Virginia. Jefferson's footprint in Napa is evident, however, from the naming of streets to the nourishing of winemaking in America. There is a generational memory in Napa that does not yet exist among the wineries of the Monticello appellation itself. Most of the wineries of the appellation are first-generation, and several have out-of-state founders. One delightful exception is Michael Bowles, proprietor of Montdomaine near Charlottesville and devoted historian of all things Jefferson and the local wine industry.

My first journey to Virginia began in 1966 when I drove there to begin graduate work at the University of Virginia. I have returned many a time, enchanted by the natural beauty of the area and the civility of its residents. My wife and I spent one week in Charlottesville in October of 2012 immersing ourselves in the local wine industry and taking refuge from Hurricane Sandy (so we literally were in a sanctuary!). While there, we were tutored on the Virginia wine industry by the gregarious Virginia wine expert Richard Leahy, who was generous in his time with us and a source of immense knowledge regarding the recent history of the Monticello appellation. Richard provided key introductions and gave us insights on the human face of the fast-growing Monticello appellation. I was impressed by the dedication, seriousness, and professionalism at all the wineries we visited that week. In conversations, I was able to develop insights into the perspectives and the passions of the people there. The excitement of the experiment of winemaking was palpable, particularly as they knew the challenges of the region and the history of Jefferson's frustrations in growing wine grapes. The compelling character of the marriage of science and art in winemaking was constantly evident. Also evident was the pride in the accomplishments of this young wine industry—something that reverberates with me as I sip Monticello appellation wines 3,000 miles away.

Appendix B has tasting notes on twelve (what else!) of my favorite Monticello appellation wines, and it is rare to experience a wine from the region that is not well rounded. The sacred geography of any wine region is composed of many terroirs, and such is the case of the Monticello appellation, where one can find windy Blue Ridge sites and soft and gentle slopes below. These terroirs comprise a chorus that defines the appellation. This chorus rarely disappoints.

Having affection for—indeed, loving—a wine region is beyond wine tourism. It does not require becoming an expert on the wineries and wines of a region any more than a lover needs a detailed psychological analysis of the loved one. What is required is simply a relationship—something beyond wine tourism but not necessarily the professionalism of a winemaker or wine critic. It is about seeing that relationship as a special bond—a sacredness that can hold you when you most need or want it. And it is about finding ways to add your own personal terroir to the terroirs of that wine region.

Wine tourism is central to the success of many wineries, including most of the wineries of the Monticello appellation. But situating your personal terroir in a sacred geography must mean more than a visit to a tasting room, an alumni reunion, a bachelorette weekend, or a wedding reception at a winery. Peter Williams, a wine marketing analyst, states: "The research identifies the need for a greater emphasis to be placed by wine tourism destinations on protecting rural landscapes, encouraging authentic and unique forms of development, and focusing imagery projection on those elements of the wine country experience which are central to the interests of wine tourists." But if you take your own personal terroir and marry it to a wine region, you have much more than wine tourism—you have a sacred geography that binds you and beckons you. Transcending wine tourism makes the experience deeper, and wineries and wine regions can thrive with a loyalty that makes a wine club seem almost primitive. The marketing language of "imagery projection" does not do justice to what can be found in a sacred geography.

But what does it really mean to take your own personal terroir and marry it to a wine region? It can be as simple as attaching each practical wisdom to a given winery so as to stimulate memory. Or it can be as complex as creating a story about your sacred geography that takes the flow of your practical wisdoms and combines it with the flow of wineries in a wine region. On a pilgrimage, where you begin and where you end are crucial. Likewise with practical wisdoms—so make your first and last as significant as you possibly can. The route is easier to see once you know the beginning and the end.

There is history in your personal terroir and in the sacred geography of your wine region. Appreciating both histories leads to mental associations that are as rich as the geography itself. With the Monticello appellation, one has not only Jefferson but the Civil War, which led to Charlottesville's being the wine capital of the South, according to Lee Reeder of Burnley Vineyards. Richard Leahy, in *Beyond Jefferson's Wines*, has told well the story of the evolution of grapes and wines in Virginia, from the nineteenth-century Norton grape to the successful reintroduction of Viognier grapes in the past twenty-five years. This renaissance in memory has not been limited to people like Leahy or historian-winemakers like Michael Bowles, quoted at the beginning of this chapter. For example, Dennis Horton of Horton Vineyards has been a leader in the rediscovery of grapes and the invention of processes that have contributed to the thriving wine industry around Charlottesville. Memory nurtures meaning, and it can be decisive in the world of practice.

In my interview of Horton in 2012, I heard something profound that I rediscovered only as I was finishing this book. Dennis spoke of "grapes that want to be here." That is why your geography is so sacred—so that you will want to discover or rediscover that special place where you want to be.

—⚭—

The flow of the last drops has taken us to what might seem to be the end, but also could be seen as a beginning. To quote the Persian poet Rumi: "One maddening drop, then another, you pour wine for us now like that." Raise a toast to the new cottabus. Enjoy—and think.

Autumn in a Virginia Vineyard

Appendix A

The Science of the 12 Drop Rule

The explanation of the 12 drop rule revolves around five factors: gravity, viscosity, wettability, the clarification-stabilization of wine, and human agency. Here I follow the famed bio-geographer Jared Diamond, whose approach to finding the simplest explanation for a phenomenon is to establish the smallest number of factors without which the phenomenon or event would not occur. These five factors are the ones I have established, but I am sure some scientists will want to refine or even refute them!

As with Newton and his apple, we need to find out why things drop down, not up. Gravity is the answer, of course, and there is no 12 drop rule without it. But the phenomenon of the last drops is complicated by the fact that there is a radical slowing as we watch for the last drops to fall. The partial explanation for this is in the notion of viscosity—that is, liquid consistency. The viscosity of wine is measured by how thick or thin it is. The higher the viscosity, the more robust the wine, and the more it will cling to the sides of a glass, producing the "legs" that wine tasters frequently observe and note—even though legs are not always associated with quality.

Gravity interacts with viscosity because when we pour, there is a different, higher-velocity pattern of fluid movement in the center of the flow than near the walls of the bottle. And the clinging of drops to the inside surface is a result of the wettability factor: the ability of a liquid to maintain contact with a solid surface when the two are brought together. Gravity is required to keep the fluid near the walls of the bottle moving—that is why one must hold the wine bottle upside down for a length of time to derive the last drops. So viscosity and wettability explain why "legs" develop and why the speed of the drops varies.

But there could not be a 12 drop rule as we know it today if sediment were a prominent feature at the bottom of a vessel of wine. Most wines, but especially reds because of their robust qualities, develop sediment as color pigments and tannins bond and particles fall to the bottom of the bottle. Decanting of wine was developed, in part, to separate wine from the sediments and is also used to let wine "breathe"—that is, interact with air to develop more aroma.

Decanting helps clarify the wine and reduces its viscosity so it can flow more freely. The processes for clarifying wine now go far beyond decanting. There are a variety of small particles in wine including pieces of grape, bacteria, proteins, tannins, and phenolic compounds that decanting alone cannot handle. Modern winemaking uses a variety of processes to clarify and stabilize wines, including fining, filtration, and flotation. Fining is a process in which a chemical agent is added to the wine to accelerate the precipitation of particles. Filtration then captures a variety of particles, especially bacteria. Flotation refers to a process of pushing bubbles of air into the bottom of a tank. As the bubbles rise, particles cling to them, and the resulting froth at the top can be skimmed away.

As for stabilization, this usually involves the near-freezing of wine before bottling. Crystallization of particles can occur, and further fining and filtration can capture even more particles, particularly proteins.

Winemakers who want to encourage long aging in a bottle may not want to thoroughly clarify or stabilize so as to promote formation of more intriguing aromas with aging. This is done often with premium red wines and can lead to sediments in the bottle. But, of course, decanting can be used to deal with this.

The fifth factor in the development of the 12 drop rule is human agency, which is both implicit and explicit in the preceding factor. Although fermentation of grapes is a natural process (occurring before humans discovered it), human agency is needed to make wine, transport it, market it, and explore the whole range of experiences and considerations associated with wine appreciation. Needless to say—but I will—it took human agency to discover the 12 drop rule. And, more significantly, it takes human agency to make more of the 12 drop rule than its discovery.

The science of the 12 drop rule, then, begins in explanation and is empirically confirmed by duplication of the exercise of counting the minimum number of drops left in a bottle of wine after normal poring. Explanation is centered on how and why drops remain; empirical confirmation is the catalyst to the 12 drop experience and to the discovery that there is more to life than what we may have believed!

Appendix B

Tasting Notes: Monticello Appellation Wines

The Monticello appellation (AVA) in Virginia markets itself as the birthplace of American wines. Below, find tasting notes on twelve representative wines from the appellation plus a thirteenth drop:Monticello Vineyards in the Napa Valley. Tasting notes are from our friends, and descriptions of the wineries are from winery websites.

1. Afton Mountain Vineyards: 2012 Festa di Bacco (40 percent Sangiovese, 15 percent Cabernet Franc, 15 percent Petit Verdot, and 30 percent merlot). This award-winning wine is balanced with fig, strawberry, clove, and other spice flavors. Winery owners Elizabeth and Tony Smith are genuine Virginians who attended local Albemarle High School, were married at the UVA chapel, and had their children at the original Martha Jefferson Hospital.

2. Barboursville Vineyards: 2009 Nebbiolo. This fine red wine is great with lamb, smoky with zest and yet dry and light. Barboursville wines "redeem the gift of a gracious, generous ground, with vintages of vivid beauty" in a delightful, historic setting.

3. Blenheim Vineyards: 2012 Petit Verdot. This is dark with good color and body but surprisingly little aroma. Goes well with a variety of foods. Owner Dave Matthews has quite a following in Virginia and even touts his winery as "dog friendly."

4. Burnley Vineyards: 2012 Norton. This classic Virginia grape is spicy, deep, earthy, and grows on you. Burnley calls itself a "Virginia farm winery" and "one of the oldest vineyards in the Monticello AVA."

5. First Colony Winery: 2012 Petit Verdot. This is a musky yet balanced wine with good, deep color and a suppleness that reflects a well-balanced, rounded wine. Winemaker Jason Hayman "took great interest in the vine to wine concept." Not only that, but he married Martha, the general manager!

6. King Family Vineyards: 2011 Viognier. This popular Virginia wine is herbaceous, with a crisp yet mellow taste and a lingering mineral feel on the tongue. This Crozet-area winery aspires to greater "complexity and balance" that "reflects the importance of terroir" in the shadows of the nearby Blue Ridge Mountains.

7. Lovingston Winery: 2012 Pinotage. This South African signature variety has a nice color, is a bit smoky, and is well balanced but slightly tannic yet very drinkable. The vineyard uses "dense planting" of 1,200 vines per acre, with fewer clusters of grapes per vine. Its philosophy: "That vine concentrates all of its energy into those fewer clusters, increasing the quality of the fruit."

8. Pippin Hill Farm & Vineyards: 2013 Viognier. This is a soft, light, citrusy wine with a strong finish. Pippin Hill, one of the newest wineries in the Charlottesville area, "reflects its

Virginian agrarian essence while offering a fresh interpretation of the classic winery."

9. Prince Michel Winery: 2012 Cabernet Franc. This is a light, herbaceous wine that is surprisingly dry, with currant flavors and a long finish. The winery's "philosophy is simple—educate others on the excellence of Virginia wine in a friendly and exciting way."

10. Stinson Vineyards: 2011 Meritage. This is a bold, ripe, almost fruity wine that is mellow and well rounded with a long finish. It is delightfully complex. Stinson has a "distinct French influence" that "takes inspiration from the 'garagiste' wineries of France."

11. Trump Winery: 2012 Viognier. This crisp, fruity, lively, yet rounded wine is youthful but balanced. It marries well with chicken. At 1,300 acres, the Trump vineyard is one of the largest in the region and is "inspired by the French wine regions of Bordeaux and Champagne."

12. Veritas Vineyard & Winery: 2010 Petit Verdot. This is a supple, spicy, yet dry wine with tobacco and berry flavors and a nice finish. The Veritas philosophy is "to make wine with the classic, old-style principles of viticulture and vinification." The wine is full bodied, as are the passion and philosophical sensibilities of the founders of the winery, Andrew and Patricia Hodson.

The Thirteenth Drop

The Corley Reserve 2011 Pinot Noir is from Monticello Vineyards in the Napa Valley. Jay Corley was a dedicated Virginian who went to California in 1969 looking for small, good sites that could elaborate

Jefferson traditions and sensibilities in the prestigious Napa region. His first Pinot Noir was produced in 1984. His Corley Reserve 2011 Pinot Noir rises to Jeffersonian expectations of achievement with a mature, supple roundness that has nice length—just like Jefferson—and a maturity that can appeal to Americans of all ideological tendencies. The winery, north of the town of Napa, has a center built on the model of Jefferson's beloved Monticello home. The birthplace of American wines has an outpost on the west coast. Mr. Jefferson would have been tickled by that.

WORKS CONSULTED

Allhoff, Fritz (ed). *Wine and Philosophy.* Malden, MA: 2008.

Barks, Coleman. *The Essential Rumi.* San Francisco: 1995.

Buber, Martin. *I and Thou.* New York: 2008.

Burstein, Andrew. *The Inner Jefferson.* Charlottesville: 1997.

Csikszentmihalyi, Mihaly. *Flow: The Psychology of Optimal Experience.* New York: 1990.

Drucker, Peter. *The Practice of Management.* New York,: 1954.

Ellis, Joseph. J. *American Sphinx: The Character of Thomas Jefferson.* New York, 1998.

FitzGerald, Edward (translator). *Rubaiyat of Omar Khayyam.* New York: 1964.

Gabler, James M. *Passions: The Wines and Travels of Thomas Jefferson.* Baltimore: 1995.

Germino, Dante. *Beyond Ideology: The Revival of Political Theory.* New York: 1967.

Gilbert, Daniel. *Stumbling on Happiness.* New York: 2005.

Gladwell, Malcolm. *Blink: The Power of Thinking Without Thinking.* New York: 2005.

Goode, Jamie. *The Science of Wine.* Berkeley: 2005.

Gopnik, Adam. *Paris to the Moon.* New York: 2001.

Greenblatt, Steven. *The Swerve: How the World Became Modern.* New York: 2011.

Haidt, Jonathan. *The Happiness Hypothesis: Finding Modern Truth in Ancient Wisdom.* New York: 2006.

Hatch, Peter. *A Rich Spot of Earth: Thomas Jefferson's Revolutionary Garden at Monticello*. New Haven: 2012.

Hawkins, David. *The Roots of Literacy*. Boulder: 2000.

Heclo, Hugh. *On Thinking Institutionally*. Boulder: 2008.

Holt, Jim. *Why Does the World Exist?* New York: 2012.

Huntington, Samuel P. *Political Order in Changing Societies*. New Haven: 1968.

Johnson, Samuel. *Major Works* (Donald Greene, ed.). Oxford: 2000.

Leahy, Richard G. *Beyond Jefferson's Vines*. New York: 2012.

Lucretius. *On the Nature of Things*. Internet Classics.

McGovern, Patrick E. *Ancient Wine: The Search for the Origins of Viniculture*. Princeton: 2003.

Meacham, Jon. *Thomas Jefferson: The Art of Power*. New York: 2012.

Moyers, Bill and Campbell, Joseph. *The Power of Myth*. New York: 1988.

Nin, Anaïs. *The Diary of Anaïs Nin*. New York: 1966.

Osborne, Lawrence. *The Accidental Connoisseur: An Irreverent Journey Through the Wine World*. New York: 2004.

Peterson, Christopher. *Pursuing the Good Life: 100 Reflections on Positive Psychology*. Oxford: 2013.

Piketty, Thomas. *Capital in the Twenty-First Century*. Cambridge: 2014.

Robinson, Andrea Immer. *Great Wine Made Simple*. New York: 2005.

Santayana, George. *Three Philosophical Poets*. Boston: 1935.

Schwartz, Barry and Sharpe, Kenneth. *Practical Wisdom: The Right Way to Do the Right Thing*. New York: 2010.

Scruton, Roger. *I Drink Therefore I Am*. London: 2010.

Seligman, Martin. *Authentic Happiness*. New York. 2002.

Simon, Herbert. *Models of Thought* Volumes 1, 2. Hartford: 1979.

Smith, Barry C. (ed.). *Questions of Taste: The Philosophy of Wine*. New York: 2007.

Standage, Tom. *A History of the World in 6 Glasses*. New York: 2005.

Taylor, Charles. *Sources of the Self: The Making of the Modern Identity*. Cambridge: 2010.

Wagar, W. Warren. *The City of Man.* Boston: 1963.

Weil, Simone. *Lectures on Philosophy.* Cambridge: 1978.

Whitehead, Alfred North. *The Function of Reason.* Princeton: 1929.